The hawk was everything I wanted to be: solitary, self-possessed, free from grief, and numb to the hurts of human life

1 3 5 7 9 10 8 6 4 2

Vintage
20 Vauxhall Bridge Road,
London SW1V 2SA

Vintage Classics is part of the Penguin Random House
group of companies whose addresses can be found at
global.penguinrandomhouse.com

 Penguin
Random House
UK

H is for Hawk first published in Great Britain by Jonathan Cape in 2014
First published in Vintage in 2015

This short edition published by Vintage in 2019

penguin.co.uk/vintage

A CIP catalogue record for this book is available from the British Library

ISBN 9781784875473

Typeset in 10.5/14.5 pt FreightText Pro
by Jouve (UK), Milton Keynes
Printed and bound in Great Britain by Clays Ltd, Elcograf S.p.A.

Penguin Random House is committed to a sustainable future for our
business, our readers and our planet. This book is made from Forest
Stewardship Council® certified paper.

Recovery
HELEN MACDONALD

VINTAGE MINIS

Contents

1 Lost

I WAS ABOUT to leave the house when the phone rang. I picked it up. Hop-skippity, doorkeys in my hand. 'Hello?' A pause. My mother. She only had to say one sentence. It was this: 'I had a phone call from St Thomas' Hospital.' Then I knew. I knew that my father had died. I knew he was dead because that was the sentence she said after the pause and she used a voice I'd never heard before to say it. Dead. I was on the floor. My legs broke, buckled, and I was sitting on the carpet, phone pressed against my right ear, listening to my mother and staring at a little ball of reindeer moss on the bookshelf, impossibly light, a buoyant tangle of hard grey stems with sharp, dusty tips and quiet spaces that were air in between them and Mum was saying there was nothing they could do at the hospital, it was his heart, I think, nothing could be done, you don't have to come back tonight, don't come back, it's a long way, and it's late, and it's

such a long drive and you don't need to come back –
and of course this was nonsense; neither of us knew
what the hell could or should be done or what this
was except both of us and my brother, too, all of us
were clinging to a world already gone.

I put down the phone. The keys were still in my
hand. In that world already gone I was going for dinner with Christina, my Australian philosopher friend,
who'd been there all along, sitting on the sofa when
the phone rang. Her white face stared at me. I told her
what had happened. And insisted we still go to the
restaurant because we'd booked a table, of course we
should go, and we did go, and we ordered, and the
food came and I didn't eat it. The waiter was upset,
wanted to know if anything was wrong. Well.

I think Christina told him. I can't remember her
doing so, but he did something quite extraordinary.
He disappeared, then reappeared at the table with an
expression of anxious concern, and a double chocolate brownie with ice-cream and a sprig of mint
stuck in the top, on the house, dusted with cocoa
powder and icing sugar. On a black plate. I stared at
it. *That is ridiculous*, I thought. Then, *What is it?* I
pulled the mint out of the ice-cream, held it up,
looked at its two small leaves and its tiny cut stem
smeared with chocolate, and thought, *This isn't going
to grow again*. Touched and bewildered that a waiter
had thought that free cake and ice-cream would

comfort me, I looked at the cut end of the mint. It reminded me of something. I groped for what it could be. And then I was back three days ago, back in Hampshire, out in the garden on a bright March weekend, wincing because I saw Dad had a nasty cut on his forearm. *You hurt yourself!* I said. *Oh, that*, he said, threading another spring onto the trampoline we were building for my niece. *Did that the other day. Can't remember how. On something or other. It'll be all right though. It'll be healed soon, it's healing fine.* That was when the old world leaned in, whispered farewells and was gone. I ran into the night. I had to drive back to Hampshire. I had to go *now*. Because the cut would not. It would not heal.

Here's a word. *Bereavement*. Or, *Bereaved. Bereft.* It's from the Old English *bereafian*, meaning 'to deprive of, take away, seize, rob'. Robbed. Seized. It happens to everyone. But you feel it alone. Shocking loss isn't to be shared, no matter how hard you try. 'Imagine,' I said, back then, to some friends, in an earnest attempt to explain, 'imagine your whole family is in a room. Yes, all of them. All the people you love. So then what happens is someone comes into the room and punches you all in the stomach. Each one of you. Really hard. So you're all on the floor. Right? So the thing is, you all share the same kind of pain, exactly the same, but you're too busy experiencing total agony to feel anything other than completely alone. *That's* what it's like!' I finished my little speech in triumph, convinced that I'd hit upon the *perfect* way to explain how it felt. I was puzzled by the pitying, horrified faces, because it didn't strike me at all that an example that put my friends' families in rooms and had them beaten might carry the tang of total lunacy.

I can't, even now, arrange it in the right order. The memories are like heavy blocks of glass. I can put them down in different places but they don't make a story. One day we were walking from Waterloo to the hospital under clouds. Breathing seemed an act of discipline. Mum turned to me, her face tight, and said, 'There'll be a time when all this seems like a bad dream.' His glasses, carefully folded, placed in my mum's outstretched hand. His coat. An envelope. His watch. His shoes. And when we left, clutching a plastic bag with his belongings, the clouds were still there, a frieze of motionless cumulus over the Thames flat as a matte painting on glass. At Waterloo Bridge we leant over Portland stone and looked at the water below. I smiled for the first time, then, I think, since the phone call. Partly because the water was sliding down to the sea and this simple physics still made sense when the rest of the world didn't. And partly because a decade before, Dad had invented a gloriously eccentric weekend side-project. He'd decided to photograph every single bridge over the Thames. I went with him, sometimes, on Saturday mornings, driving up into the Cotswolds. My dad had been my dad, but also my friend, and a partner in crime when it came to quests like this. From the grassy source near Cirencester we walked and explored, followed a wormy, muddy stream, trespassed to take photos of planks over it, got shouted at by farmers, menaced by cattle, pored over maps in fierce concentration. It took a year. He did it, in the end. Every single bridge. Somewhere in the files of slides back at my mum's house is a complete photographic record of ways to cross the Thames from source to sea.

On another day, the panic was that we might not find his car. He'd parked it somewhere near Battersea Bridge and, of course, had never returned. We looked for it for hours, increasingly desperate, searching back streets and side streets and cul-de-sacs to no avail, widening our search to streets miles from anywhere we knew the car could possibly be. As the day drew on, we understood that even if we found it, Dad's blue Peugeot with his press pass tucked in the sun-visor and his cameras in the boot, our search would still have been hopeless. Of course it had been towed away. I found the number, called the compound and said to the man on the phone that the owner of the vehicle couldn't collect it because he was dead. He was my father. That he didn't mean to leave the car there but he died. That he really didn't mean to leave it. Lunatic sentences, deadpan, cut from rock. I didn't understand his embarrassed silence. He said, 'Sorry, oh God. I'm so sorry', but he could have said anything at all and it would have signified nothing. We had to take Dad's death certificate to the compound to avoid the towing fee. This also signified nothing.

After the funeral I went back to Cambridge. I didn't sleep. I drove around a lot. I stared at the sun going down and the sun coming up, and the sun in between. I watched the pigeons spreading their tails and courting each other in stately pavanes on the lawn outside my house. Planes still landed, cars still drove, people still shopped and talked and worked. None of these things made any sense at all. For weeks I felt I was made of dully burning metal. That's what it was like; so much so that I was convinced, despite all evidence to the contrary, that if you'd put me on a bed or a chair I would have burned right through.

It was about this time a kind of madness drifted in. Looking back, I think I was never truly mad. More mad north-north-west. I could tell a hawk from a handsaw always, but sometimes it was striking to me how similar they were. I knew I wasn't *mad* mad because I'd seen people in the grip of psychosis before, and that was madness as obvious as the taste of blood in the mouth. The kind of madness I had was different. It was quiet, and very, very dangerous. It was a madness designed to keep me sane. My mind struggled to build across the gap, make a new and inhabitable world. The problem was that it had nothing to work with. There was no partner, no children, no home. No nine-to-five job either. So it grabbed anything it could. It was desperate, and it read off the world wrong. I began to notice curious connections between things. Things of no import burst into extraordinary significance. I read my horoscope and believed it. Auguries. Huge bouts of déjà vu. Coincidences. Memories of things that hadn't happened yet. Time didn't run forwards any more. It was a solid thing you could press yourself against and feel it push back; a thick fluid, half-air, half-glass, that flowed both ways and sent ripples of recollection forwards and new events backwards so that new things I encountered, then, seemed souvenirs from the distant past. Sometimes, a few times, I felt my father must be sitting near me as I sat on a train or in a café. This was comforting. It all was. Because these were the normal madnesses of grief. I learned this from books. I bought books on grieving, on loss and bereavement. They spilled over my desk in tottering piles. Like a good academic, I thought books were for answers. Was it reassuring to be told that everyone sees ghosts? That everyone stops eating? Or can't stop eating? Or that grief comes in stages that can be numbered and pinned like beetles in boxes? I read that after denial comes grief. Or anger. Or guilt. I remember worrying about which stage I was at. I wanted to taxonomise the process, order it, make it sensible. But there was no sense, and I didn't recognise any of these emotions at all.

Weeks passed. The season changed. The leaves came, the mornings filled with light, the swifts returned, screaming past my Cambridge house through the skies of early summer and I began to think I was doing fine. *Normal grief*, they call it. That's what this was. An uneventful, slow climb back into life after loss. *It'll be healed soon.* I still break into a wry smile thinking of how blithely I believed this, because I was so terribly wrong. Unseen need was motoring out through me. I was ravenous for material, for love, for anything to stop the loss, and my mind had no compunction in attempting to recruit anyone, anything, to assist. In June I fell in love, predictably and devastatingly, with a man who ran a mile when he worked out how broken I was. His disappearance rendered me practically insensible. Though I can't even bring his face to mind now, and though I know not only why he ran, but know that in principle he could have been anyone, I still have a red dress that I will never wear again. That's how it goes.

Then the world itself started to grieve. The skies

broke and it rained and rained. The news was full of inundations and drowned cities; lost villages at the bottom of lakes; flash floods spilling over the M4 motorway to strand holiday traffic; kayaks on town streets in Berkshire; rising sea levels; the discovery that the English Channel was carved out by the bursting of a giant superlake millions of years ago. And the rain continued, burying the streets in half an inch of bubbling water, breaking shop canopies, making the River Cam a *café-au-lait* surge, thick with broken branches and sodden undergrowth. My city was apocalyptic. 'I don't see the weather as odd at all,' I remember saying to a friend under a café awning while the rain struck the pavement behind our chairs with such violence that we sipped coffee in cold mist.

As the rain fell and the waters rose and I struggled to keep my head above them, something new began. I'd wake up frowning. I'd dreamed of hawks, again. I started dreaming of hawks all the time. Here's another word: *raptor*, meaning 'bird of prey'. From the Latin *raptor*, meaning 'robber', from *rapere*, meaning 'seize'. Rob. Seize. The hawks were goshawks, and one in particular. A few years earlier, I'd worked at a bird-of-prey centre right at the edge of England before it tips into Wales; a land of red earth, coal-workings, wet forest and wild goshawks. This one, an adult female, had hit a fence while hunting and knocked herself out. Someone had picked her up, unconscious, put her in a cardboard box and brought her to us. Was anything broken? Was she damaged? We congregated in a darkened room with the box on the table and the boss reached her gloved left hand inside. A short scuffle, and then out into the gloom, her grey crest raised and her barred chest feathers puffed up into a meringue of aggression and fear, came a huge old female goshawk. Old because her feet were gnarled and dusty, her eyes a deep, fiery orange, and she was *beautiful*. Beautiful like a granite cliff or a thundercloud. She completely filled the room. She had a massive back of sun-bleached grey feathers, was as muscled as a pit bull, and intimidating as hell, even to staff who spent their days tending eagles. So wild and spooky and reptilian. Carefully, we fanned her great, broad wings as she snaked her neck round to stare at us, unblinking. We ran our fingers along the narrow bones of her wings and shoulders to check nothing was broken, along bones light as pipes, hollow, each with cantilevered internal struts of bone like the inside of an aeroplane wing. We checked her collarbone, her thick, scaled legs and toes and inch-long black talons. Her vision seemed fine too: we held a finger in front of each hot eye in turn. *Snap, snap*, her beak went. Then she turned her head to stare right at me. Locked her eyes on mine down her curved black beak, black pupils fixed.

Then, right then, it occurred to me that this goshawk was bigger than me and more important. And much, much older: a dinosaur pulled from the Forest of Dean. There was a distinct, prehistoric scent to her feathers; it caught in my nose, peppery, rusty as storm-rain.

Nothing was wrong with her at all. We took her outside and let her go. She opened her wings and in a second was gone. She disappeared over a hedge slant-wise into nothing. It was as if she'd found a rent in the damp Gloucestershire air and slipped through it. That was the moment I kept replaying, over and over. That was the recurring dream. From then on, the hawk was inevitable.

2 Small worlds

I WAS TWELVE years old when I first saw a trained goshawk. *Please, please, PLEASE!* I'd begged my parents. They let me go. Drove me there, even. *We'll look after her*, the men said. They carried hawks on their fists: orange-eyed goshawks as remote and composed as statuary, with barred grey tails and breast feathers of vermiculated snow. I couldn't speak. I wanted my parents to leave. But when their car pulled away I wanted to run after it. I was terrified. Not of the hawks: of the falconers. I'd never met men like these. They wore tweed and offered me snuff. They were clubbable men with battered Range Rovers and vowels that bespoke Eton and Oxford, and I was having the first uncomfortable inklings that while I wanted to be a falconer more than anything, it was possible I might not be *entirely* like these men; that they might view me as a curiosity rather than a kindred spirit. But I pushed my fears aside in favour of silence, because it was the first time I'd ever seen falconry in the field. *I'll remember this day for ever*, I thought. *One day this will be me.*

We walked in dark winter light over fields furred with new wheat. Vast flocks of fieldfares netted the sky, turning it to something strangely like a sixteenth-century sleeve sewn with pearls. It was cold. My feet grew heavy with clay. And twenty minutes after we'd set out, it happened – the thing I expected, but for which I was entirely unprepared. A goshawk killed a pheasant. It was a short, brutal dive from an oak into a mess of wet hedge; a brief, muffled crash, sticks breaking, wings flapping, men running, and a dead bird placed reverently in a hawking bag. I stood some way off. Bit my lip. Felt emotions I hadn't names for. For a while I didn't want to look at the men and their hawks any more and my eyes slipped to the white panels of cut light in the branches behind them. Then I walked to the hedge where the hawk had made her kill. Peered inside. Deep in the muddled darkness six copper pheasant feathers glowed in a cradle of blackthorn. Reaching through the thorns I picked them free, one by one, tucked the hand that held them into my pocket, and cupped the feathers in my closed fist as if I were holding a moment tight inside itself. It was death I had seen. I wasn't sure what it had made me feel.

But there was more to that day than my first sight

of death. There was something else, and it also gave me pause. As the afternoon wore on, men started disappearing from our party. One by one their hawks had decided they wanted no more of proceedings, saw no good reason to return to their handlers, and instead sat in trees staring out over acres of fading pasture and wood, fluffed and implacable. At the end of the day we left with three fewer men and three fewer hawks, the former still waiting beneath their hawks' respective branches. I knew goshawks were prone to sulk in trees: all the books had told me so. 'No matter how tame and loveable,' I'd read in Frank Illingworth's *Falcons and Falconry*, 'there are days when a goshawk displays a peculiar disposition. She is jumpy, fractious, unsociable. She may develop these symptoms of passing madness during an afternoon's sport, and then the falconer is in for hours of annoyance.'

These men didn't seem annoyed; fatalistic merely. They shrugged their waxed cotton shoulders, filled and lit pipes, waved the rest of us farewell. We trudged on into the gloom. There was something of the doomed polar expedition about it all, a kind of chivalric Edwardian vibe. *No, no, you go on. I'll only slow you down.* The disposition of their hawks was peculiar. But it wasn't unsociable. It was something much stranger. It seemed that the hawks couldn't see us at all, that they'd slipped out of our world entirely and moved into another, wilder world from which humans had been utterly erased. These men knew they had vanished. Nothing could be done except wait. So we left them behind: three solitary figures staring up into trees in the winter dusk, mist thickening in the fields around them, each trusting that the world would later right itself and their hawk would return. And like the feathers in my pocket, their waiting also tugged at my faintly baffled heart.

I never forgot those silent, wayward goshawks. But when I became a falconer I never wanted to fly one. They unnerved me. They were things of death and difficulty: spooky, pale-eyed psychopaths that lived and killed in woodland thickets. Falcons were the raptors I loved: sharp-winged, bullet-heavy birds with dark eyes and an extraordinary ease in the air. I rejoiced in their aerial verve, their friendliness, their breathtaking stoops from a thousand feet, wind tearing through their wings with the sound of ripping canvas. They were as different from hawks as dogs are from cats. What's more, they seemed *better* than hawks: my books all assured me that the peregrine falcon was the finest bird on earth. 'She is noble in her nature' wrote Captain Gilbert Blaine in 1936. 'Of all living creatures she is the most perfect embodiment of power, speed and grace.' It took me years to work out that this glorification of falcons was partly down to who got to fly them. You can fly a goshawk almost anywhere, because their hunting style is a quick dash from the fist after prey at close range, but to fly falcons properly you need space: grouse moors, partridge manors, huge expanses of open farmland, things not easy to come by unless you're wealthy or well connected. 'Among the cultured peoples,' Blaine wrote, 'the use and possession of the noble falcons were confined to the aristocracy, as an exclusive right and privilege.'

Compared to those aristocratic falconers, the *austringer*, the solitary trainer of goshawks and sparrowhawks, has had a pretty terrible press. 'Do not house your graceless austringers in the falconers' room,' sniped the fourteenth-century Norman writer Gace de la Bigne. 'They are cursed in scripture, for they hate company and go alone about their sport. When one sees an ill-formed man, with great big feet and long shapeless shanks, built like a trestle, hump-shouldered and skew-backed, and one wants to mock him, one says, "Look, what an austringer!"' And as the austringer, so the hawk, even in books written six centuries later. 'One cannot feel for a goshawk the same respect and admiration that one does for a peregrine,' Blaine explained. 'The names usually bestowed upon her are a sufficient index to her character. Such names as "Vampire", "Jezebel", "Swastika" or even "Mrs Glasse" aptly fit her, but would ill become a

peregrine.' Goshawks were ruffians: murderous, difficult to tame, sulky, fractious and foreign. *Bloodthirsty*,
wrote nineteenth-century falconer Major Charles
Hawkins Fisher, with patent disapproval. *Vile*. For
years I was inclined to agree, because I kept having
conversations that made me more certain than ever
that I'd never train one. 'You fly falcons?' a falconer
enquired of me once. 'I prefer goshawks. You know
where you are with a gos.'

'Aren't they a pain in the arse?' I said, remembering all those hunched forms lodged high in wintry
trees.

'Not if you know the secret,' he countered, leaning
closer. There was a slight Jack Nicholson vibe to all
this. I drew back, faintly alarmed. 'It's simple. If you
want a well-behaved goshawk, you just have to do
one thing. Give 'em the opportunity to kill things.
Kill as much as possible. *Murder* sorts them out.' And
he grinned.

'Right,' I said. There was a pause, as if it wasn't
quite the right response. I tried again. 'Thanks.' And
I was all, *Bloody hell! I'm sticking with falcons, thank
you very much*. I'd never thought I'd train a goshawk.
Ever. I'd never seen anything of myself reflected in
their solitudinous, murderous eyes. *Not for me*, I'd
thought, many times. *Nothing like me*. But the world
had changed, and so had I.

———

It was the end of July and I'd convinced myself that I was pretty much back to normal. But the world around me was growing very strange indeed. The light that filled my house was deep and livid, half magnolia, half rainwater. Things sat in it, dark and very still. Sometimes I felt I was living in a house at the bottom of the sea. There were imperceptible pressures. Tapping water-pipes. I'd hear myself breathing and jump at the sound. Something else was there, something standing next to me that I couldn't touch or see, a thing a fraction of a millimetre from my skin, something vastly *wrong*, making infinite the distance between me and all the familiar objects in my house. I ignored it. *I'm fine*, I told myself. *Fine*. And I walked and worked and made tea and cleaned the house and cooked and ate and wrote. But at night, as rain pricked points of orange light against the windows, I dreamed of the hawk slipping through wet air to somewhere else. I wanted to follow it.

I sat at my computer in my rain-lit study. I telephoned friends. I wrote emails. I found a hawk-breeder in Northern Ireland with one young goshawk left from that year's brood. She was ten weeks old, half Czech, one-quarter Finnish, one-quarter German, and she was, for a goshawk, small. We arranged that I should drive to Scotland to pick her up. I thought that I would like to have a small goshawk. 'Small' was the only decision I made. I didn't think for a second there was any choice in the matter of the hawk itself. The hawk had caught me. It was never the other way around.

When the rain stopped the heat began. Dogs panted flat in the black shade under the limes, and the lawns in front of the house paled and burned to hay. A damp, hot wind pushed leaves about but failed to cool anything; it was a wind that made things worse, like stirring a hot bath with your hand. Walking in it was like wading neck-deep through thick liquid. I struggled into the furnace of my car and drove to a friend's house in a village just outside the city. I wanted to talk goshawks, and there was no one better than Stuart to do it with. He is my goshawk guru. Years ago I'd hawked with him on late winter afternoons, crunched across long shadow and sugar-beet in search of wild fenland pheasants, his big old female gos sitting on his fist like a figurehead, leaning into the gilded wind. He is a splendid chap; a carpenter and ex-biker, solid and serene as a mid-ocean wave, and his partner Mandy is brilliantly generous and funny, and seeing them both was such a shot in the arm. I'd halfway forgotten how kind and warm the world could be. Stuart fired up the barbecue, and the garden filled with kids and teenagers and cigarette smoke and pointers nosing around, and ferrets rattling in their hutches, and the sky grew whiter as the afternoon went on, and the sun turned gauzy behind a spreading mat of fibrous cloud. A Spitfire banked overhead. We mopped our brows. The dogs panted, the ferrets drank from their water bottles, and Stuart slaved over his barbecue, coming back around the side of the house wiping his forehead on his arm. 'It's getting cooler!' he said, surprised. 'No, you've walked away from the barbecue!' we chorused.

I plonked myself down with a burger on a white plastic chair. And there, on a perch on the lawn, shaded by the hedge and ignoring the melee, was a perfect little peregrine, carefully preening the long, flippy barred feathers of his undercarriage. 'Half-Czech?' Stuart was saying. 'The most bloody-minded gos I ever trained was Czech. It was a *nightmare*. Are you *sure* you want to do this?' He tipped his head towards the bird on the lawn. 'You can fly that if you like,' he said. 'Want a peregrine?'

My heart skipped a beat. The falcon. There he was, an impossibly beautiful creature the colour of split flint and chalk, wings crossed sharp over his back, his dark, hooded face turned up to the sky. He was watching the Spitfire overhead with professional curiosity. I looked up at the plane. Its engine note had changed; it was throttling back, slowly descending through white air to the aviation museum where it lived. The peregrine bobbed his head, watching it too. Our gazes were exactly aligned. For a long, sinking moment, I wondered if I was making a terrible mistake.

'I'd love to,' I said stiffly, formally, the half-burger in my hand suddenly unappetising. One deep breath, then, and the words came. 'I mean, *normally* I would, I'd leap at the chance; that's an amazing offer, Stu. But I really do want this gos.' He nodded. Manfully, I finished the burger. Ketchup dripped down my arm like a wound.

3 Holding tight

WHEN YOU ARE broken, you run. But you don't always run away. Sometimes, helplessly, you run towards. It was a morning in early August, and I was four hundred miles from home. What I was doing felt like a drugs deal. It certainly looked like one. For minutes on end I'd paced up and down a Scottish quayside with a can of caffeinated soda in one hand, a cigarette in the other, and an envelope stuffed with £800 in twenty-pound notes in my back pocket. Over there in the car sat Christina, spectacularly impassive in a pair of aviator shades. She'd come along to keep me company, and I hoped she wasn't bored. She was probably bored. Perhaps she was asleep. I walked back to the car. It was my father's. I was driving it now, but the boot was full of things I couldn't bring myself to remove: 35mm film canisters; a crushed packet of aspirin; a newspaper with a half-finished crossword in my father's hand; a pair of winter gloves.

I leaned against the bonnet, rubbed my eyes and looked out at the harbour, willing the ferry into view. A clear pool of turquoise was spreading out there over the Irish Sea; small crosses that were gulls traversed it. It seemed strange that it was day at all; both of us were wiped out from yesterday's long drive, and faintly freaked out by the hotel we'd stayed at the night before. *21st Century Hotel!* it said on a laminated paper sign by the door. When we opened it the first thing we saw was a plastic bulldog sitting on a desk, grimacing at us with the malevolent, merry belligerence of a thing from a nightmare.

In the hotel room we found a broken computer, a sink that wasn't plumbed in, and a fully functioning cooker we'd been instructed not to use under any circumstances. 'Health and Safety,' the hotelier had explained, rolling his eyes. There were, unexpectedly, two televisions, acres of brown suedette stapled to the walls, and a bathroom with a six-foot sunken bath into which Christina subsided, marvelling at the tea-tinted peat water. I collapsed into a chair, the journey running in my mind like a road-movie directed by a drug-addled auteur. Giant Irn-Bru trucks full of orange, bubblegum-flavoured fizzy Scottish soda. A raven standing in a puddle by the side of the road, wet-trousered and chisel-beaked. Motorway service station A. Motorway service station B. A sandwich. A large cup of undrinkable coffee. Endless miles. More skies. A near-accident caused by inattention on a hillside somewhere. Motorway service stations C and D. I massaged my aching right calf, blinked away the after-images, and got to making jesses.

I should have made them before, but I couldn't. Only now did the hawk seem real enough to make them necessary. Jesses are the soft leather straps that fit through the leather anklets on a trained hawk's legs. Singular, *jess*. It's a French word from the fourteenth century, back when falconry was the favourite game of the ruling elite. A little scrap of social history in the name for a strip of leather. As a child I'd cleaved to falconry's disconcertingly complex vocabulary. In my old books every part of a hawk was named: wings were *sails*, claws *pounces*, tail a *train*. Male hawks are a third smaller than the female so they are called *tiercels*, from the Latin *tertius*, for *third*. Young birds are *eyasses*, older birds *passagers*, adult-trapped birds *haggards*. Half-trained hawks fly on a long line called a *creance*. Hawks don't wipe their beaks, they *feak*. When they defecate they *mute*. When they shake themselves they *rouse*. On and on it goes in a dizzying panoply of terms of precision. The terms were precise for a reason. Knowing your falconry terminology attested to your place in society. Just as in the 1930s T. H. White worried about whether a hunting crop should be properly called a hunting whip, or a riding crop, or a riding whip, or just a crop, or a whip, so in the sixteenth century the Jesuit spy Robert Southwell was terrified he'd be found out because he kept forgetting his falconry terms. But the words weren't about social fear when I was small. They were magic words, arcane and lost. I wanted to master this world that no one knew, to be an expert in its perfect, secret language.

You can buy it all on the internet now: jesses, hoods, bells, gloves, everything. But when I began falconry, most of us made our own equipment. We'd buy swivels from deep-sea-fishing shops, leashes from ships' chandlers, beg offcuts from leather tanneries and shoe factories to make our own jesses and hoods. We adapted, we adopted, we usually didn't improve. Certainly I didn't. I spent countless hours waxing cotton thread, punching holes in my hands instead of leather in error, frowning, wiping blood away, trying again and again to cut and make and sew things that looked like the photographs in books, waiting for the glorious day when I might have a hawk of my own.

I have a suspicion that all those hours making jesses and leashes weren't just preparation games. In a scrapbook of my childhood drawings is a small pencil sketch of a kestrel sitting on a glove. The glove's just an outline, and not a good one – I was six when I drew it. The hawk has a dark eye, a long tail, and a tiny fluffy spray of feathers under its hooked beak. It is a happy kestrel, though a ghostly one; like the glove, it is strangely transparent. But one part of it has been carefully worked: its legs and taloned toes, which are larger than they ought to be, float above the glove because I had no idea how to draw toes that gripped. All the scales and talons on all the toes are delineated with enormous care, and so are the jesses around the falcon's legs. A wide black line that is the leash extends from them to a big black dot on the glove, a dot I've gone over again and again with the pencil until the paper is shined and depressed. It is an anchor point. *Here*, says the picture, *is a kestrel on my hand. It is not going away. It cannot leave.*

It's a sad picture. It reminds me of a paper by the psychoanalyst D. W. Winnicott, the one about a child obsessed with string; a boy who tied together chairs and tables, tied cushions to the fireplace, even, worryingly, tied string around his sister's neck. Winnicott saw this behaviour as a way of dealing with fears of abandonment by the boy's mother, who'd suffered bouts of depression. For the boy, the string was a kind of wordless communication, a symbolic means of joining. It was a denial of separation. *Holding tight.* Perhaps those jesses might have been unspoken attempts to hold on to something that had already flown away. I spent the first few weeks of my life in an incubator, full of tubes, under electric light, skin patched and raw, eyes clenched shut. I was the lucky one. I was tiny, but survived. I had a twin brother. He didn't. He died soon after he was born. I know almost nothing about what happened, only this: it was a tragedy that wasn't ever to be spoken of. It was a time when that's what hospitals told grieving parents to do. Move on. Forget about it. Look, you have a child! Get on with your lives. When I found out about my twin many years later, the news was surprising. But not *so* surprising. I'd always felt a part of me was missing; an old, simple absence. Could my obsession with birds, with falconry in particular, have been born of that first loss? Was that ghostly kestrel a grasped-at apprehension of my twin, its carefully drawn jesses a way of holding tight to something I didn't know I'd lost, but knew had gone? I suppose it is possible.

But now my father had died. *Hold tight.* I hadn't ever imagined that making jesses could be a symbolic act. But as I sat there, cutting hide into long strips, soaking them in warm water, stretching them, greasing them with leather dressing, turning them this way and that in this strange room of broken objects, I knew they were more than just pieces of leather. These were the cords that would hold me to the hawk, just as they would hold the hawk to me. I picked up the craft knife and tapered the end of one jess to a point with a long, smooth cut. *There.* I was conjuring presences, doing this. Suddenly the hawk was very real. And so, in a burst of remembrance so fierce he could have been there in the room, was my father. Grey hair, glasses, blue cotton shirt, a tie slightly askew, a cup of coffee in one hand and a look of amusement on his face. He used to make me cross by calling falconry equipment by the wrong names. He'd call hoods *hats*. Creances, *bits of string*. He did it on purpose. I'd get cross and correct him, thinking he was teasing me.

And now I saw that Dad had known exactly what these things were called, but in the world of the photo-journalist, the more expert you were, the less likely you were to call anything by its proper name. For him, photographs were *snaps*. Cameras simply *kit*. It wasn't ever teasing. He was paying me a compliment. Bloody fourteenth-century French vocabulary. Shit. Shit shit *shit*. It wasn't his way at all. My throat hurt. My eyes hurt too, and my heart. I cut the end of the other jess. Shaking fingers. Then I placed the two jesses side by side on the glass tabletop. They matched. *Tomorrow*, I thought, *I'm meeting a man I don't know off the Belfast ferry and I'm going to hand him this envelope full of paper in exchange for a box containing a goshawk*. It seemed the unlikeliest thing imaginable.

The goshawk I was about to collect had been bred in an aviary near Belfast. Breeding goshawks isn't for the faint-hearted. I've had friends who've tried it and shaken their heads after only one season, scratching their newly greyed hair in a sort of post-traumatic stupor. 'Never again', they say. 'Ever. Most stressful thing I've ever done.' Try it, and you discover there's a very fine line between goshawk sexual excitement and terrible, mortal violence. You have to watch your hawks constantly, monitor their behaviour, ready yourself for intervention. It's no good just putting a couple of goshawks in an aviary and leaving them to it. More often than not the female will kill her mate. So instead you house them in separate but adjoining solid-walled aviaries, with a barred hatch between the two through which the pair can see each other. As winter turns to spring they conduct their courtship, like Pyramus and Thisbe, through the gap in the wall, calling, displaying, dropping their powder-blue wings and fluffing their white undertail coverts that look for all the world like a pair of capacious marabou bloomers, and only when the female seems ready – a piece of fine judgement that does not admit error – do you let the male into the breeding chamber. If all goes well, they mate, lay eggs, and a new generation of home-bred goshawks, downy white chicks with bleary eyes and tiny talons, enters the world. I'd never met the breeder of my new hawk, but I knew already he was a man of steel nerves and superhuman patience.

———

Time passed on the Scottish quay and brightness moved in from the sea. Then a man was walking towards us, holding two enormous cardboard boxes like a couple of oversized suitcases. Strangely alien suitcases that didn't seem to obey the laws of physics, because as he walked they moved unpredictably, in concert neither with his steps nor with gravity. *Whatever is in them is moving*, I thought with a little thump of my heart. He set the boxes down, ran his hand through his hair. 'I'm meeting another falconer here in a bit. He's having the younger bird. Yours is the older. Bigger too,' he said. 'So.' He ran his hand through his hair again, exposing a long talon scratch across his wrist, angry at its edges and scurfed with dried blood. 'We'll check the ring numbers against the Article 10s,' he explained, pulling a sheaf of yellow paper from the rucksack and unfolding two of the official forms that accompany captive-bred rare birds throughout their lives. 'Don't want you going home with the wrong bird.'

We noted the numbers. We stared down at the boxes, at their parcel-tape handles, their doors of thin plywood and hinges of carefully tied string. Then he knelt on the concrete, untied a hinge on the smaller box and squinted into its dark interior. A sudden *thump* of feathered shoulders and the box shook as if someone had punched it, hard, from within. 'She's got her hood off,' he said, and frowned.

That light, leather hood was to keep the hawk from fearful sights. Like us.

Another hinge untied. Concentration. Infinite caution. Daylight irrigating the box. Scratching talons, another thump. And another. *Thump.* The air turned syrupy, slow, flecked with dust. The last few seconds before a battle. And with the last bow pulled free, he reached inside, and amidst a whirring, chaotic clatter of wings and feet and talons and a high-pitched twittering and it's all happening at once, the man pulls an enormous, *enormous* hawk out of the box and in a strange coincidence of world and deed a great flood of sunlight drenches us and everything is brilliance and fury. The hawk's wings, barred and beating, the sharp fingers of her dark-tipped primaries cutting the air, her feathers raised like the scattered quills of a fretful porpentine. Two enormous eyes. My heart jumps sideways. She is a conjuring trick. A reptile. A fallen angel. A griffon from the pages of an illuminated bestiary. Something bright and distant, like gold falling through water. A broken marionette of wings, legs and light-splashed feathers. She is wearing jesses, and the man holds them. For one awful, long moment she is hanging head-downward, wings open, like a turkey in a butcher's shop, only her head is turned right-way-up and she is seeing more than she has ever seen before in her whole short life. Her world was an aviary no larger than a living room. Then it was a box. But now it is this; and she can see *everything*: the point-source glitter on the waves, a diving cormorant a hundred yards out; pigment flakes under wax on the lines of parked cars; far hills and the heather on them and miles and miles of sky where the sun spreads on dust and water and illegible things moving in it that are white scraps of gulls. Everything startling and new-stamped on her entirely astonished brain.

Through all this the man was perfectly calm. He gathered up the hawk in one practised movement, folding her wings, anchoring her broad feathered back against his chest, gripping her scaled yellow legs in one hand. 'Let's get that hood back on,' he said tautly. There was concern in his face. It was born of care. This hawk had been hatched in an incubator, had broken from a frail bluish eggshell into a humid perspex box, and for the first few days of her life this man had fed her with scraps of meat held in a pair of tweezers, waiting patiently for the lumpen, fluffy chick to notice the food and eat, her new neck wobbling with the effort of keeping her head in the air. All at once I loved this man, and fiercely. I grabbed the hood from the box and turned to the hawk. Her beak was open, her hackles raised; her wild eyes were the colour of sun on white paper, and they stared because the whole world had fallen into them at once. *One, two, three.* I tucked the hood over her head. There was a brief intimation of a thin, angular skull under her feathers, of an alien brain fizzing and fusing with terror, then I drew the braces closed. We checked the ring numbers against the form.

It was the wrong bird. This was the younger one. The smaller one. This was not my hawk.

Oh.

So we put her back and opened the other box, which was meant to hold the larger, older bird. And dear God, it did. Everything about this second hawk was different. She came out like a Victorian melodrama: a sort of madwoman in the attack. She was smokier and darker and much, much bigger, and instead of twittering, she wailed; great, awful gouts of sound like a thing in pain, and the sound was unbearable. *This is my hawk*, I was telling myself and it was all I could do to breathe. She too was bareheaded, and I grabbed the hood from the box as before. But as I brought it up to her face I looked into her eyes and saw something blank and crazy in her stare. Some madness from a distant country. I didn't recognise her. *This isn't my hawk.* The hood was on, the ring numbers checked, the bird back in the box, the yellow form folded, the money exchanged, and all I could think was, *But this isn't my hawk.* Slow panic. I knew what I had to say, and it was a monstrous breach of etiquette. 'This is really awkward,' I began. 'But I really liked the first one. Do you think

there's any chance I could take that one instead . . . ?'
I tailed off. His eyebrows were raised. I started again,
saying stupider things: 'I'm sure the other falconer
would like the larger bird? She's more beautiful than
the first one, isn't she? I know this is out of order, but
I . . . Could I? Would it be all right, do you think?'
And on and on, a desperate, crazy barrage of inco-
herent appeals.

I'm sure nothing I said persuaded him more than
the look on my face as I said it. A tall, white-faced
woman with wind-wrecked hair and exhausted eyes
was pleading with him on a quayside, hands held out
as if she were in a seaside production of *Medea*. Looking at me he must have sensed that my stuttered
request wasn't a simple one. That there was something behind it that was very important. There was a
moment of total silence.

'All right,' he said. And then, because he didn't see
me believe him, 'Yes. Yes, I'm sure that'll be OK.'

4 The rite of passage

THE FEATHERS DOWN her front are the colour of sunned newsprint, of tea-stained paper, and each is marked darkly towards its tip with a leaf-bladed spearhead, so from her throat to her feet she is patterned with a shower of falling raindrops. Her wings are the colour of stained oak, their covert feathers edged in palest teak, barred flight-feathers folded quietly beneath. And there's a strange grey tint to her that is felt, rather than seen, a kind of silvery light like a rainy sky reflected from the surface of a river. She looks new. Looks as if the world cannot touch her. As if everything that exists and is observed rolls off like drops of water from her oiled and close-packed feathers. And the more I sit with her, the more I marvel at how reptilian she is. The lucency of her pale, round eyes. The waxy yellow skin about her Bakelite-black beak. The way she snakes her small head from side to side to focus on distant objects. Half the time she seems as alien as a snake, a thing hammered of metal and scales and glass. But then I see ineffably birdlike things about her, familiar qualities that turn her into something loveable and close. She scratches her fluffy chin with one awkward, taloned foot; sneezes when bits of errant down get up her nose. And when I look again she seems neither bird nor reptile, but a creature shaped by a million years of evolution for a life she's not yet lived. Those long, barred tail-feathers and short, broad wings are perfectly shaped for sharp turns and brutal acceleration through a world of woodland obstacles; the patterns on her plumage will hide her in perfect, camouflaging drifts of light and shade. The tiny, hair-like feathers between her beak and eye – *crines* – are for catching blood so that it will dry, and flake, and fall away, and the frowning eyebrows that lend her face its hollow rapacious intensity are bony projections to protect her eyes when crashing into undergrowth after prey.

Everything about the hawk is tuned and turned to hunt and kill. Yesterday I discovered that when I suck air through my teeth and make a squeaking noise like an injured rabbit, all the tendons in her toes instantaneously contract, driving her talons into the glove with terrible, crushing force. This killing grip is an old, deep pattern in her brain, an innate response that hasn't yet found the stimulus meant to release it. Because other sounds provoke it: door hinges, squealing brakes, bicycles with unoiled wheels – and on the second afternoon, Joan Sutherland singing an aria on the radio. *Ow*. I laughed out loud at that. Stimulus: *opera*. Response: *kill*. But later these misapplied instincts stop being funny. At just past six o'clock a small, unhappy wail came from a pram outside the window. Straight away the hawk drove her talons into my glove, ratcheting up the pressure in savage, stabbing spasms. *Kill*. The baby cries. *Kill kill kill.*

Two days pass. I sit and walk, and sit and sleep, the hawk almost constantly on my fist. My arm aches and a damp tiredness grips my heart. A farming programme on the radio. Wheat, borage, rapeseed. Polytunnels and cherries. The hawk is alternately a hunchback toad, a nervous child or a dragon. The house is a tip. Scraps of raw meat decorate the bin. I've run out of coffee. I have forgotten how to speak. My mouth makes small, mumbled assurances to the hawk that all is well. She meets them with silence, with thready, nervous cheeps through her nose. As I walk she follows my feet with her eyes as if they were two small animals moving about the house with us. She is interested in flies, in specks of floating dust, in the way light falls on certain surfaces. What is she looking at? What is she thinking? I hear the click of the nictitating membrane that crosses her eyes as she blinks, and now I see them closely her eyes begin to disturb me. They look like discs of pale paper stuck to the side of her head, each with a hole-punched black pupil housed under a transparent dome like a bubble of water. The hawk is stranger than I'd thought. And calmer than I'd believed possible.

I'm starting to worry. Is there something wrong with her? She's oddly tame. Where is the lunatic I'd expected? For two days I've sat with her and not once have I longed to dismember her and batter her to death. I'd expected a barrelling tornado of terror and wildness, some great and awful struggle of souls, but instead, as the light deepens and the late swifts outside ascend on flickering wings to bury themselves in the sky, I sit on a sofa watching a tired hawk go to sleep. The leading edges of her wings drop and rest against the glove. One downy grey eyelid slides up to cover an eye, then the other. Her shoulders fall; her head wobbles. The tip of her glossy black beak sinks into the feathers over her crop. Watching her doze in this vesper hour my eyes close too, but when sleep comes I am standing in the skeleton of a burned-out house, in white, blank air that glitters faintly with mica or frost. Around me are blackened joists and rafters. I put out a hand. Touch a piece of charred wood. Cold, furred, wrong. Rising panic. Refusal. A sense of absolute dismay. Then of toppling, the house collapsing into itself and on top of me. And we wake together, the hawk and I, her with a start of apprehension, a tightening of feet and feathers, and me with a slow, sickening disorientation that makes me fasten desperately onto the sight of the hawk to drag me back into a world with no ash in it. The same thoughts over and over. Why is she sleeping so much? Hawks sleep when they're sick. She must be sick. Why am I sleeping? Am I sick too? What is wrong with her? What is wrong with us?

Nothing was wrong with the hawk. She wasn't sick. She was a baby. She fell asleep because that's what babies do. I wasn't sick either. But I was orphaned and desperately suggestible, and I didn't know what was happening to me. I'd flown scores of hawks, and every step of their training was familiar to me. But while the steps were familiar, the person taking them was not. I was in ruins. Some deep part of me was trying to rebuild itself, and its model was right there on my fist. The hawk was everything I wanted to be: solitary, self-possessed, free from grief, and numb to the hurts of human life.

I was turning into a hawk.

I didn't shrink and grow plumes like the Wart in *The Sword in the Stone*, who was transformed by Merlyn into a merlin as part of his magical education. I had loved that scene as a child. I had read it over and over again, thrilling at the Wart's toes turning to talons and scratching on the floor, his primary feathers bursting in soft blue quills from the end of his fingers. But I was turning into a hawk all the same.

The change came about through my grief, my watching, my not being myself. The first few days with a wild new hawk are a delicate, reflexive dance of manners. To judge when to scratch your nose without offence, when to walk and when to sit, when to retreat and when to come close, you must read your hawk's state of mind. You do this by watching her posture and her feathers, the workings of which turn the bird's shape into an exquisitely controlled barometer of mood. A hawk's simpler emotions are easily perceived. Feathers held tight to the body mean *I am afraid*. Held loosely they mean *I am at ease*. But the longer you watch a hawk the more subtleties you see; and soon, in my hypervigilant state, I was responding to the tiniest of cues. A frowning contraction of the crines around her beak and an almost imperceptible narrowing of her eyes meant something like *happy*; a particular, fugitive expression on her face, oddly distant and reserved, meant *sleepy*.

To train a hawk you must watch it like a hawk, and so you come to understand its moods. Then you gain the ability to predict what it will do next. This is the sixth sense of the practised animal trainer. Eventually you don't see the hawk's body language at all. You seem to feel what it feels. Notice what it notices.

The hawk's apprehension becomes your own. You are exercising what the poet Keats called your chameleon quality, the ability to 'tolerate a loss of self and a loss of rationality by trusting in the capacity to recreate oneself in another character or another environment'. Such a feat of imaginative recreation has always come easily to me. Too easily. It's part of being a watcher, forgetting who you are and putting yourself in the thing you are watching. That is why the girl who was me when I was small loved watching birds. She made herself disappear, and then in the birds she watched, took flight. It was happening now. I had put myself in the hawk's wild mind to tame her, and as the days passed in the darkened room my humanity was burning away.

Three tentative raps on the front door. 'Hang on,' I call. A small voice inside me, resentful and savage, hisses, *Go away*. It is Christina with two takeaway coffees and the Sunday papers. 'So,' she says, settling herself in a chair by the fireplace. 'How's it going? Is the hawk OK?' I nod. I raise my eyebrows. I am vaguely aware this isn't enough to make a conversation. 'Mmm,' I say. The voice is not entirely mine. She hugs her knees and looks at me curiously. *I must try harder*, I think. So I talk about the hawk for a while, and then I can't speak any more. I stare at my paper cup.

I'm pleased to see her. *She shouldn't be here.* This coffee is good. *We should be alone.* These resentful thoughts surprise me. Manning the hawk is all about showing it new things. Christina is a new thing. 'I'm going to try something,' I tell her. 'Ignore the hawk. Just keep reading the papers.' I fetch a fresh piece of beef from the kitchen, sit with the hawk on the sofa, reach up and remove her hood. There's a moment of fast-beating incomprehension and the air in the room turns to ice. Tight-feathered, in savage irreso-lution, eyes like porcelain saucers, the hawk stares. My heart sinks. She is going to bate. But the moment stretches, and she does not. After a deal of cautious observation she decides that a human turning news-paper pages is something entirely fascinating.

An hour later all is calm and companionable. We're watching television. The hawk balances evenly on the balls of her feet, mesmerised by the flickering screen. Tiny white wisps of down still attached to the finials of her scapular feathers wave in the draught from the hall. Then, without warning, she bursts from my fist in a whirlwind of a bate. Papers fly. Christina flinches. *Shit*, I think. *I should hood her, let her rest. This is too much*. But I am wrong. Fear did not engender this bate. Frustration did. She picks at her jesses in dis-placed fury, then tears at the meat beneath her toes. She is hungry. The food is a wonderful discovery. She is a delicate, decisive gastronome. She picks, and bites, and swallows, and squeaks in happiness, and bites and swallows again. I am thrilled. But also indignant. This moment was to have been born of solitude and meditative darkness. Not this. Not daylight with another person in the room and 'Allo 'Allo! on the television. Not in the presence of comedy Nazis and a soundtrack about giant sausages and the occupation of France. She narrows her eyes with pleasure, bristles around the nose, and her feathers soften into loose falls of ochre and cream. 'Has she done that before?' asks Christina. 'No,' I say. 'This is the first time.' Laughter from the television audience as an SS officer dressed as a woman hoves into view and the hawk finishes eating, lifts herself into a vast, frothy mop of feathers, holds them there for an instant and shakes them all back into place. A rouse. It is a sign of contentment. She has not roused before.

Now my hawk is tame enough to sit bareheaded. From her perch by the window she watches the curtains move over a carpet furred with dust. She won't yet be picked up without a bate. But I'm working on that. From the sofa I flick a thumbnail-sized scrap of steak towards her. It falls with a sticky *thwick* on the vinyl cloth beneath her perch. She looks down at it. Frowns. Turns her head to one side to inspect it more carefully. Then hops down with a scratch of talons and a rattle of feathers, picks the meat delicately from the floor and swallows it. Gone. For a while she stands there, as if trying to remember something she has forgotten, then bounces back onto the perch with brio, all shaggy trousers and waggy tail. I wait a while, then send another scrap of flesh her way. *Thwick. Hop. Swallow. Hop.* I lower myself to the floor and sit there for a while. Shuffling slowly sideways on my rump, I watch the hawk out of the corner of my eye. She tenses. I stop. She untenses. I move. She tenses. I stop again. I inch across the carpet until I reach that hair-fine juncture where any movement nearer will make her bate from the perch. Breathing as carefully as if I were about to take an extravagantly long rifle-shot, I slowly – so slowly – extend my garnished fist towards her. I can almost taste the hawk's indecision; the air is thick with it. But – joy! – she is looking at the food in front of her. She leans forward as if to pick it from the glove, but then something inside her snaps. With an awful clang of the metal ring of the perch against its steel base, she bates away from me. *Damn.* I take her up onto the glove for a few mouthfuls of food.

When she is settled back on her perch, we play the game again. *Flick. Hop. Flick.* She's solved the puzzle of where the food is coming from and some part of her is reconsidering my place in her world. She watches me intently as I inch towards her and again extend the garnished glove. She leans across and snaps up my gift of steak. My heart leaps. She takes another piece, and then another, smacking her glossy black chops.

As I sit there happily feeding titbits to the hawk, her name drops into my head. *Mabel*. From *amabilis*, meaning loveable, or dear. An old, slightly silly name, an unfashionable name. There is something of the grandmother about it: antimacassars and afternoon teas. There's a superstition among falconers that a hawk's ability is inversely proportional to the ferocity of its name. Call a hawk *Tiddles* and it will be a formidable hunter; call it *Spitfire* or *Slayer* and it will probably refuse to fly at all. My hawk needed a name as far from Death as it could get. 'Mabel.' I say the word out loud to her and watch her watching me say it. My mouth shapes the word. 'Mabel.' And as I say it, it strikes me that all those people outside the window who shop and walk and cycle and go home and eat and love and sleep and dream – all of them have names. And so do I. 'Helen,' I say. How strange it sounds. How very strange. I put another piece of meat on my glove and the hawk leans down and eats.

5 For whom the bell

'BLOODY HELL, SHE'S calm, Helen,' Stuart says. 'I can feel her heartbeat. She's not bothered at all.' His head is bowed low over the table, fingers spread wide over the closed wings of my hooded hawk. He holds her upon a kitchen cushion as firmly and as gently as if she were made of glass. 'Good,' I say, shifting her covert feathers carefully aside to reveal the base of her tail. Here, just before the long feathers join her body, the quills are hollow and translucent, and I'm about to glue and tie a bell the size and shape of an acorn onto the topmost pair. It doesn't take long. I tug on it gently to check it is secured, then take the hawk back onto my fist. She rouses and the bell sounds loud in the bright room. It does not seem to concern her at all.

Bells are among the most ancient of falconry technologies. For years I'd bought bells from Pakistan, hand-hammered from brass to a design of immense antiquity, but the one Mabel wears is American; modern, small and light, handmade from nickel silver. When she flies free it will tell me where she is. Bells were traditionally attached to hawks' legs on tiny leather straps called bewits, but a tail-mounted bell is much better for a goshawk, for they have an invariable habit of shaking their tails when they land. You can stand with your back to a tree with a gos in it and trace its movements from branch to branch behind you through sound alone.

But bells aren't foolproof: their sound is dulled by wind and distance, and a motionless hawk is silent, so when Mabel flies free she'll also wear a tiny radiotransmitter, and I'll carry the receiver that picks up its signal over my back in a black cloth case. Even with these double precautions the thought of taking her off the creance fills me with dread. I had never lost a hawk. I'd never expected to. But once she is free, I'm convinced that Mabel will rocket away from me and disappear for ever. I'm even more certain of this when I fly her a few hours later. This time she doesn't even snatch at the food in my glove, just flies straight past me until she's brought down to earth.

Disconsolate, I carry her back to the edge of the village playing fields. Stuart watches me approach, looks critically at the hawk. He rubs the back of his neck with one hand. His face, tanned and lined by years of sun and wind, is thoughtful and grave.

'It might be the bell, do you think?' I say. 'Freaked her out a bit?'

He frowns. 'It's a new place, too. But she's not ready yet, Helen. Not yet.' He feels her breastbone speculatively. 'She needs to come down more. She's still too fat. You're feeding her rabbit? Just rabbit?'

I nod miserably.

He looks at me, considering. 'Tell you what, Helen, come out on the hill with me tomorrow,' he says. 'I'll be going up there to fly the tiercel. We'll get her out into the fields, away from streets and houses. She needs space.'

'That would be brilliant, Stuart.'

'I'll pick you up at five.'

'Thank you. Thank you so much.'

'She needs to come down a bit more, Helen.'

He was offering to help, and I was unprepared for how this made me feel. I'd flown scores of hawks. I'd taught falconry to beginners. I'd written papers on it, had lectured on its venerable history. But now I bowed my head before Stuart. He knew what to do. He knew about goshawks and I did not. I felt weak with relief at not having to be an expert any more. There he was, rolling a cigarette, reassuringly calm and kind, a proper, generous friend; and it was there, standing on the edge of a village playing field, that I gratefully stepped into novicehood again, as if I had never seen a hawk in my life.

Stuart pulls off the road onto a farm track to the west of the city. The evening is warm, but there's a torn-paper whiteness behind the sun that speaks of frost to come. I unhood the hawk. Her pale eyes stare out across a hillside of stubble and chalky till, at slopes cut with hedgerows crisped at their edges into shot-silk taffeta. She sees skeletal teasels and fencewires. Larks calling overhead. A discarded twelve-gauge shotgun cartridge by my feet. *Red*. She glances down at it, then up, fixing her gaze on something three fields away, delighted at this enlargement of her world. When Stuart takes her upon his fist she leans back and stares up at him with almost comical dread, head sunk deep into her shoulders. But soon she relaxes; for all his strangeness there is a kindness to him, an ease and proficiency in his dealings with her that quickly reassures. We unwind the creance and call her across the bare field. She flies badly, of course. I see that flinch as she approaches, that moment where all conviction and trust slides away and I am revealed to her as a monster. Once again I grab the creance and bring her to earth. Her feet sink into the friable loam; she looks down in wonderment at her half-obscured toes.

Stuart is firm with me. Tells me she needs to be keener. I cannot bear it. I get him to swear that my hawk won't die in the night.

'Of course she won't,' he says, blue eyes crinkling into something between a smile and a frown.

'Are you *sure*?' I say pathetically. I am horribly worried that I am starving her to death.

He extends a hand and feels Mabel's breastbone, her ribcage, the muscles under her wings.

'She's *fine*, Helen.'

'Honestly?'

'*Yes.*'

I trudge back to the car, staring down at my feet. Then Stuart stops dead.

'Stuart?'

'Look!' he says. 'Look at that!'

'What?' I say, turning and shading my eyes. 'I can't see anything.'

'Look towards the sun.'

'I am!'

'Look *down*!'

Then I see it. The bare field we'd flown the hawk upon is covered in gossamer, millions of shining threads combed downwind across every inch of soil. Lit by the sinking sun the quivering silk runs like light on water all the way to my feet. It is a thing of unearthly beauty, the work of a million tiny spiders searching for new homes. Each had spun a charged silken thread out into the air to pull it from its hatch-place, ascending like an intrepid hot-air balloonist to drift and disperse and fall. I stare at the field for a long time. It reminds me of an evening last autumn on a trip to Uzbekistan. I'd been sitting on the ground outside my tent wondering if the terrible smell was a decomposing cow, or something much worse. Before me were miles of marsh and desert and in the far distance the Fergana Mountains, fading into haze. Then I saw the strangest things hanging in the air, and I could not work out what they were. They looked like white question marks, and they dis-obeyed the laws of physics alarmingly. There was no wind at all, yet they hovered, and sank, and rose with supernatural slowness. What the hell? I ran after one. I walked up to it so that it was within six inches of my nose, and I still couldn't understand what it was. It was as long as my hand from wrist to finger-tip; it was white, and squiggly like the doodle you make with a running-out pen, and made of some material I couldn't identify. I thought of manna, and soda, of ash and silly string. And then I looked very, very closely, as it rose very, very slowly upwards, and there, from the base of this white frothy squiggle, was an almost-invisible line. And right at the bottom of the line was a spider exactly this size, the size of the word *Ah*.

———

The next day I left Mabel at home and took a train to London. I didn't want to leave her, and I didn't want to go. I remembered the city after my father's death as a ghastly place, pale and caustic under toppling clouds. But now, rounding the corner of Fleet Street, I found the city wasn't empty any more. It was a dark and fathomless warren of litter and glass, bankers and traders streaming through its sunken lanes. Sills, barricades, alleys. Tipping gutters, anti-pigeon spikes, pavements patterned with spots of trodden gum. And then, suddenly, St Bride's Church, caged behind railings on a raised platform of green-stained stone. The picture editor of my father's newspaper was there, waiting with my mother and brother at the door. I had not met him before. Blue eyes in a fierce, sad pugilist's face, a strong hand-shake, a pinstripe suit. He'd set up this meeting: the newspaper was organising a memorial service for my father, and we'd come here to discuss it with the canon of the church. And so in the vestry office we talked of hymns, of invitations, of readings and speakers and songs. I said I would make a speech. We talked some more. My mother sat very upright in a grey sweater and pink gilet, her hair carefully brushed, her face taut and pale. *Oh Mum*. James was even paler. He shot me a tight smile. My eyes prickled and burned. He turned to the canon. 'I work as a designer,' he said. 'I could design the Order of Service?' The canon nodded and pushed a handful of printed booklets across the desk towards us. 'These are from past services,' he said, dipping his head in a gesture of unconscious, anxious tenderness. 'They might help you with your father's?' I picked up the nearest. On its cover was a smiling middle-aged stranger in a piano-keyboard tie. I looked at his face for a long time, pressing the pad of one finger hard into the corner of the stiff cover to make a tiny flare of pain to cover the ache in my heart.

When we got up to leave the canon pressed business cards into our hands. Business cards. *Absurd.* The tie. The incongruity. *This. All this.* I looked back at the office. Striplights and pinboards, coat-hooks and fax machines. Diaries and schedules. The offices of death. I felt laughter rising inside me. I tried to stifle it. It came out as a broken cough. This had happened before; once, on the morning Mum and I had to choose my father's coffin, sitting in wing-back armchairs in the undertaker's office before a small vase of salmon-coloured roses. Dim light. A cramped room. A stifling hush. The undertaker handed us a laminated folder, and it fell open onto a page of coffins painted with football colours, with photorealistic spitfires, golf-courses, saxophones and trains. We'd laughed then as I laughed now. The coffins, like the tie, made the small loves of life ridiculous in death, the business card made the memorial mundane. The laughter was because there was no way of incorporating these signs of life into the fact of death. I laughed because there was nothing else I could do.

On the way home I felt a great and simple sadness. I missed my dad. I missed him very much. The train curved and sunlight fell against the window, obscuring the passing fields with a mesh of silver light. I closed my eyes against the glare and remembered the spider silk. I had walked all over it and had not seen it. I had not known it was there. It struck me then that perhaps the bareness and wrongness of the world was an illusion; that things might still be real, and right, and beautiful, even if I could not see them – that if I stood in the right place, and was lucky, this might somehow be revealed to me. And the sun on the glass and the memory of the shining field, and the awful laughter, and the kindness of that morning's meeting must have thinned the armour of silence I'd worn for months, because the anger was quite gone now, and that evening as we drove to the hill, I said in a quiet voice, 'Stuart, I'm not dealing very well with things at the moment.'

I said, 'I think I'm a bit depressed.'

'You've lost your father, Helen,' he said.

'I'm training a gos. I suppose it's quite stressful.'

'You've *lost your father*. And you're doing OK with the gos,' he added. 'You might not see it, but you are.

She'll be flying free, soon. She's nearly there, Helen. Don't be so hard on yourself.'

I hadn't told him everything. I hadn't confessed the unpaid bills, the letters from the bank, the impossible nights, the mornings in tears. But I had told him something. I looked at Mabel. Her head drooped forward. She looked indescribably mournful in her hood. I stroked her craggy, snake-scale toes. She was asleep. I touched the hood, very gently, and felt the whole weight of her sinking, sleeping head against my fingers. *Perhaps I should ask Stuart to take us home*, I thought. I was so impossibly tired; there seemed no point in flying her at all. But when I unhooded her out on the hill, Stuart, noticing her oddly upright stance, the pale feathers fluffed over her toes, the rising feathers on her crown, the shackly, possessive grasp of her feet on the glove, raised his eyebrows and asked, 'What does she weigh?'

'One pound and fifteen ounces.'

'Look at her,' he said. 'She's a different hawk today.'

She was. I called her. I had lost hope in her coming but I called her all the same. And she flew to me. She flew like a promise finally kept. She raced towards me, wings flickering across fifty yards of flint-strewn earth, hit the glove and stayed. I gave her back to Stuart and called her again. Three times she flew to my fist the whole length of the creance with total conviction. There was no hesitation, no faltering. The hawk flew to me as if I were home.

'You've hit her flying weight,' Stuart said approvingly. 'A couple more days of this and we'll get her flying free.' Of course he was right. I had miscalculated her flying weight for weeks. But the narcissism of the bereaved is very great. I thought that the reason the hawk had flown to me was because I had confessed how bad things were. It had made me feel better – and it was this that had made me less offputting to my hawk. *I must try to be happier*, I told myself. *For the hawk's sake I must.*

6 Extinction

FALCONERS HAVE A word for hawks in the mood to slay: they call the bird *in yarak*. The books say it comes from the Persian *yaraki*, meaning power, strength and boldness. Much later I was amused to find that in Turkish it means an archaic weapon and is also slang for penis: never doubt that falconry is a boys' game. As I carry Mabel up the stony track to the hill each day I watch her come into yarak. It is disturbingly like watching her slow possession by a demon. Her crest feathers rise, she leans back, tummy feathers fluffed, shoulders dropped, toes very tight on the glove. Her demeanour switches from *everything scares me* to *I see it all; I own all this and more*.

In this state she's a high-tension wire-strung hawk of murderous anticipation, wound so tight she bates at anything that moves – things she's not a hope of catching: flocks of larks, distant racing pigeons, even a farmyard tomcat – and I hold her jesses tight and don't let her go. But when a hen pheasant rockets up from my feet I do. She chases it fiercely but it has too much of a head start; after fifty yards she slows, turns in mid-air and comes back to me, planing over the top of a hedgerow ash to land gently upon my fist. On another day she bursts downhill in pursuit of a rabbit and is about to grab it when the rabbit stops dead in its tracks. She overshoots and crashes into the ground; the rabbit jinks, doubles back on itself and runs uphill to the safety of a hole. She leaps back into the air to resume her pursuit but the rabbit is gone. She alights, confused and crestfallen, on the grass.

I'm crestfallen too. It's not that I'm baying for blood. But I don't want Mabel to get discouraged. In the wild, young goshawks will sit for hours hidden in trees waiting for an easy opportunity to present itself: a fledgling crow, a baby rabbit. But it is September now: nature's easy pickings are grown. And while most goshawkers have a dog to help them find game, or a ferret to bolt rabbits for their hawk to chase, I do not. All I can do is walk with the hawk and hope we find something to catch. But I am a liability; her senses are far better than mine. We walk past a gully under a hedge where there are rabbits and rats and God knows what, all covered with brambles and briars and robins' pincushions set on briar stems like exotic fruit, their vegetable hairs brushed green and rose and carmine. She dives from my fist towards the undergrowth. I don't know she's seen something – so I don't let her go. Then I curse my pathetic human senses. Something was there. A mouse? A pheasant? A rabbit? With a stick I poke about in the gully but nothing comes out. It is too late; whatever it was has gone. We walk on. Mabel stops looking murderous and assumes an expression of severe truculence. *How the hell*, I imagine her thinking, *am I supposed to catch things with this idiot in tow?*

I return exhausted from our latest attempt: a hellish, traumatic afternoon, fractious, gusty and sour. I'd met Stuart and Mandy out on the hill. 'I'll run the dogs for you,' he said. 'See if we can get a point for her.' But Mabel wasn't having any of it. She bated and twittered and glared. She hated the dogs, she hated it all. I hated it too. I fed her up and drove us home. Then I started pulling clothes from a wardrobe, attempting to transform myself into a cheerful, civilised person who does things like go to art galleries. I brush the burrs from my hair, wash my face, shrug on a skirt, push the sleeves of a cashmere jumper back to my elbows, paint a black line over each eyelid. Foundation. Mascara. A smear of lipsalve to seal my wind-dried mouth, a pair of shiny boots with heels that make me worry that I can't run in them – for running seems essential these days – and I check the result in a mirror. It is a good disguise.

I'm pleased with how convincing it seems. But it's getting late, and I'm running against the clock. I have twenty minutes to get to a gallery for the opening of an art exhibition. I'm supposed to give a talk about it in a few weeks' time and I have to see the bloody thing first. I battle with sleep as I drive, and by the time I reach the gallery doors my knees are ready to give way.

I expect a room of paintings and sculpture. But when I open the doors there's something so unexpected inside my brain turns cartwheels. It is a full-sized bird hide built of rough-hewn pine, and it is – I read the sign – an exact copy of a real structure in California. Seeing it in the gallery is as disconcerting as opening a fridge door and finding a house within. The hide is dark inside and packed with people peering through a window in one wall. I look out of it too. *Oh!* I see the trick. It is a neat one. The artist has filmed the view from the real hide, and is projecting it onto a screen beyond the window. It shows a soaring California condor, a huge, dusty-black carrion-eating vulture rendered nearly extinct by persecution, habitat destruction and poisoning from lead-contaminated carcasses. By the late 1980s only twenty-seven birds remained, and in a last-ditch effort to save the species they were trapped and taken into captivity so that their domestic-bred young could be used to repopulate the wild. Some people tried to stop this happening. They believed honestly and sincerely that once all the birds were captive, condors would cease to exist. These birds are made of wildness, they argued. A captive condor is a condor no more.

I watch the condor for a while. It makes me impatient. My head is packed with real skies and real hawks. I'm remembering live condors I'd met at a captive-breeding centre years before: vast, loose-feathered, turkey-necked birds with purpose and curiosity; avian hogs in black feather-boas. Precious, yes, but complicated, real, idiosyncratic, astonishing. The condor on the gallery screen was nothing like them. *Helen, you are an idiot*, I think. *That is the whole point of this exhibition. The whole point of it, right there in front of you.*

I think of what wild animals are in our imaginations. And how they are disappearing – not just from the wild, but from people's everyday lives, replaced by images of themselves in print and on screen. The rarer they get, the fewer meanings animals can have. Eventually rarity is all they are made of. The condor is an icon of extinction. There's little else to it now but being the last of its kind. And in this lies the diminution of the world. How can you love something, how can you fight to protect it, if all it means is loss? There is a vast difference between my visceral, bloody life with Mabel and the reserved, distanced view of modern nature-appreciation. I know that some of my friends see my keeping a hawk as morally suspect, but I couldn't love or understand hawks as much as I do if I'd only ever seen them on screens. I've made a hawk part of a human life, and a human life part of a hawk's, and it has made the hawk a million times more complicated and full of wonder to me. I think of my chastened surprise when Mabel played with a paper telescope. She is real. She can resist the meanings humans give her. But the condor? The condor has no resistance to us at all. I stare at the attenuated, drifting image on the gallery screen. It is a shadow, a figure of loss and hope; it is hardly a bird at all.

The other exhibit is perfectly simple. It is a bird lying on its back in a glass box in an empty room. Seeing it makes all my soapbox musings fade and fall away. It's a parrot, a Spix's macaw. There are none left in the wild now and the last captive birds are the focus of desperate attempts to keep the species alive. This one is long dead. Stuffed with cotton wool, a small paper label tied to one of its clenched dry feet, its feathers are the deep blue of an evening sea. It might be the loneliest thing I have ever seen. But leaning over this spotlit skin in a glass coffin, I don't think of animal extinction at all. I think of Snow White. I think of Lenin in his ill-lit mausoleum. And I think of the day after my father died, when I was shown into a hospital room where he lay.

But this isn't him, I thought, wildly, after the woman closed the door. *He isn't here.* Someone had dressed a waxwork of my father in hospital pyjamas and a patterned duvet. Why would they do that? It made no sense. It was nonsense. I took a step back. Then I saw on his arm the cut that would not heal and stopped. I knew I had to speak. For ages I could not. Physically could not. Something the size of a fist was in my throat and it was catching the words and not letting them out. I started to panic. Why couldn't I speak? *I have to speak to him.* Then the tears came. They were not like normal tears. Water coursed in sheets down my cheeks and dripped to the hospital floor. And with the water came words. So I leaned over the bed and spoke to my father who was not there. I addressed him seriously and carefully. I told him that I loved him and missed him and would miss him always. And I talked on, explaining things to him, things I cannot now remember but which at the time were of clear and burning importance. Then there was silence. And I waited. I did not know why. Until I realised it was in hope that an answer might come. And then I knew it was over. I took my father's hand in my own for the last time, squeezed it in a brief goodbye and quietly left the room.

The next day out on the hill Mabel learns, I suppose, what she is for. She chases a pheasant. It crashes into the brambles beneath a tall hedge. She lands on top of the hedge, peering down, her plumage bright against the dark earth of the further slope. I start running. I think I remember where the pheasant has gone. I convince myself it was never there at all. I know it is there. Clay sticks to my heels and slows me down. I'm in a world of slowly freezing mud, and even the air seems to be getting harder to run through. Mabel is waiting for me to flush the pheasant, if only I knew where it was. Now I am at the hedge, trying to find it, constructing *what will happen next* scenarios in my head, and at this point they're narrowing fast, towards point zero, when the pheasant will fly. I cannot see Stuart and Mandy any more, though I know they must be there. I'm crashing through brambles and sticks, dimly aware of the catch and rip of thorns in my flesh. Now I cannot see the hawk because I am searching for the pheasant, so I have to work out what she is doing by putting myself in her mind – and so I become both the hawk in the branches above and the human below. The strangeness of this splitting makes me feel I am walking under myself, and sometimes away from myself. Then for a moment everything becomes dotted lines, and the hawk, the pheasant and I merely elements in a trigonometry exercise, each of us labelled with soft italic letters. And now I am so invested in the hawk and the pheasant's relative positions that my consciousness cuts loose entirely, splits into one or the other, first the hawk looking down, second the pheasant in the brambles looking up, and I move over the ground as if I couldn't possibly affect anything in the world. There is no way I can flush this pheasant. I'm not here. Time stretches and slows. There's a sense of panic at this point, a little buffet of fear that's about annihilation and my place in the world. But then the pheasant is flushed, a pale and burring chunk of muscle and feathers, and the hawk crashes from the hedge towards it. And all the lines that connect heart and head and future possibilities, those lines that also connect me with the hawk and the pheasant and with life and death, suddenly become safe, become tied together in a small muddle of feathers and gripping talons that stand in mud in the middle of a small field in the middle of a small county in a small country on the edge of winter.

I stare at the hawk as she grips the dead pheasant, and her mad eyes stare right back at me. I'm amazed. I don't know what I expected to feel. Bloodlust? Brutality? No. Nothing like that. There are thorn-scratches all over me from where I dived through the hedge, and an ache in my heart I can't place. There's a sheeny fog in the air. Dry. Like talc. I look at the hawk, the pheasant, the hawk. And everything changes. The hawk stops being a thing of violent death. She becomes a child. It shakes me to the core. She is a child. A baby hawk that's just worked out who she is. What she's for. I reach down and start, unconsciously as a mother helping a child with her dinner, plucking the pheasant with the hawk. For the hawk. And when she starts eating, I sit on my heels and watch, watch her eat. Feathers lift, blow down the hedge, and catch in spiders' webs and thorn branches. The bright blood on her toes coagulates and dries. Time passes. Benison of sunlight. A wind shifts the thistle stalks and is gone. And I start crying, soundlessly. Tears roll down my face. For the pheasant, for the hawk, for Dad and for all his patience, for that little girl who stood by a fence and waited for the hawks to come.

7 Apple Day

OH GOD. WHAT am I doing here? I'm sitting on a white plastic picnic chair under the shade of a marquee roof. Ten feet behind me Mabel resembles a shadow cast on water; her wings are crossed as tight as swords and her eyes bloom huge with horror. I know how she feels. *Too many people*, I think, fidgeting on my seat. *Too many people.*

'So, Helen,' Stuart had said. 'The landowner's asked us to bring some hawks along for Apple Day at the farm.'

'Apple Day?'

Stuart told me that it was a tiny country fair, a celebration of rural history, farming and local food. 'We're not flying, just weathering the hawks in a marquee so members of the public can see them. I'll take my tiercel. Greg's bringing his barbary. Alan's coming up with some eagles. Can you bring Mabel?'

'Yes, of course,' I said. 'No problem.' I could do

this. I'd worked in a falconry centre, for God's sake. All I did for months was show people hawks. But as the day drew closer I started to fret. *How will Mabel cope?* Two months ago she was a bomb-proof, crowd-proof goshawk. But goshawks aren't like other hawks: they need constant carriage to stay tame. We've not seen people for weeks. She's forgotten how not to be scared of people. *And so have I.* My teeth are clenched so tight in the face of the crowds I feel pain blossoming up my jaw.

After twenty minutes Mabel raises one foot. It looks ridiculous. She is not relaxed enough to fluff out her feathers; she still resembles a wet and parti-coloured seal. But she makes this small concession to calmness, and she stands there like a man driving with one hand resting on the gearstick. She looks pathetically small next to the birds beside her. To her left is a golden eagle, a hulking great thing with chest-feathers like armoured scales and taloned feet the size of human hands. To her right is a male martial eagle, an antelope-killing black and white monster with piercing white eyes. It is enormous, bigger than most of the dogs walking past the mesh fence in front of the marquee, and it watches them go by with its black chrysanthemum-petalled crest raised in idle speculation of murder.

Stuart has brought his tiercel peregrine. Greg has brought his barbary falcon, a tiny jewelled dusty-blue and copper falcon with thin golden toes. While it preens he sits cross-legged, chatting with members of the public, his red cashmere jumper holed wildly at the elbow. Alan the eagle-man is drinking tea from a plastic cup, resting an arm on the tall perch of a saker falcon, which looks up at him with a mild and playful eye.

I can't sit still. I go for a walk round the fair. It is not very big, but it is full of surprising things. Smoke from an oil-drum barbecue curling through drying chestnut leaves. Beneath the tree an ancient wooden cider press pouring apple juice into cups. The crushed apples fall into mounds of oxidising pulp beside it and the man working the mechanism is shouting something to the craggy plantsman on the next stand with stripling trees for sale. I find a cake stand, a face-painting stand, a stand of vivaria full of snakes, spiders and stick insects the size of your hand. A stall of orange pumpkins by an ice-cream van. A boy kneeling by a hutch staring at a rabbit under a paper sign that says MY NAME IS FLOPSEY. 'Hello, Flopsey,' he says, bringing his hand up to the wire. I walk into a white marquee, and inside, in dim green shade, find trestle-tables displaying hundreds of apple varieties. Some are the size of a hen's egg; some are giant, sprawling cookers you'd need two hands to hold. Each variety sits in a labelled wooden compartment. I walk slowly along the apples, glorying in their little differences. Soft orange, streaked with tiger-spots of pink. *Charles Ross. Berkshire pre 1890. Dual use.* A little one with bark-like blush markings over a pale green ground. *Coronation. Sussex 1902. Dessert.* Miniature green boulders, the side in shadow deep rose. *Chivers Delight. Cambridgeshire 1920. Dessert.* Huge apple, deep yellow with hyperspace-spotting of rich red. *Peasgood's Nonsuch. Lincolnshire 1853. Dual use.*

The apples cheer me. The stalls have too. I decide the fair is a wonderful thing. I wander back to my chair, and as Mabel relaxes, so do I. I wolf down a burger, gossip with my falconer friends. Stories are told, jokes are made, old grievances aired, the qualities and abilities and flights of various hawks discussed in minute detail. It strikes me suddenly how much British falconry has changed since the days of Blaine and White. Back then it was the secretive, aristocratic sport of officers and gentlemen. In Germany, falconry had fed into the terrible dreams of an invented Aryan past. Yet here we are now in all our variousness. A carpenter ex-biker, a zookeeper ex-soldier, two other zookeepers, an electrician and an erstwhile historian. Four men, two women, two eagles, three falcons and a goshawk. I swig from a bottle of cider and this company is suddenly all I'd ever wished for.

'Excuse me? Is that a goshawk?'

He's in his forties, with glasses. A thickset, cheerful man holding a wriggling toddler. 'Hang on, Tom,' he says. 'We're going to get an ice-cream. I just want to talk to this lady for a second.'

I grin. I know how it feels to hold onto a creature who wants to be somewhere else. And then my heart falters, just a little.

No father, no partner, no child, no job, no home.

Get over yourself, Helen, I hiss inwardly.

'It's yours?' he says. 'Wow.'

I tell him about the goshawk. He listens. Then his face turns serious and sad.

'You are so lucky,' he says. 'I've always wanted to do falconry. All my life. I've got books and everything. But I've never had the time.' There's a pause. 'Maybe one day.' He hugs Tom a little closer. 'Come on then, you,' he says, and they walk away to the ice-cream van.

White air and aching bones. Another migraine. I swallow a dose of codeine and paracetamol. My head still hurts. There's a brumous, pewter light outside, as if someone had stuck tracing paper against the glass. I go back to bed. *Must fly goshawk,* I think when I wake. *Must fly goshawk.* But I'm finding it so hard to move that secretly I'm hoping the hawk's weight is wrong, or the weather is. I have no excuse to stay in bed this time: both hawk and weather are fine.

We drive into a strange, windless, sunny afternoon that makes everything resemble hollow metal models painted with enamel. Clouds, swags of leaves, houses. All in the same plane, like a stage-set, and riveted together. The air smells of woodsmoke. I am inexpressibly tired. I park the car on the grassy verge near the field, change Mabel's jesses, unhood her, and she snaps into yarak in an instant. She knows where she is. And here we are. And there are the rabbits. She leaves the fist. As soon as she does the pain in my head recedes and my exhaustion fades. Her flight is getting much more stylish. I am still astonished by how fast she is. When I watch her scaly, foreshortened, hunched flight away from me towards a distant target, I swear that the world around her slows. She seems to be moving at precisely the right speed, and everything around her – rabbits running, leaves falling, a pigeon flying overhead, all these things slow down as if they're moving through liquid.

I am becoming fascinated by her quality of attention. I'm starting to believe in what Barry Lopez has called 'the conversation of death', something he saw in the exchange of glances between caribou and hunting wolves, a wordless negotiation that ends up with them working out whether they will become hunter and hunted, or passers-by. I am wondering whether my goshawk does this. Mabel back on the fist, I walk towards three rabbits. They are sitting on the grass, right there, no more than ten yards away.

Closer. Five yards! Mabel is in raging yarak, but is ignoring them. She's staring with interest at the other end of the field. Something out there, a good six or seven seconds' flight away. 'Mabel!' I murmur. 'Look!' And I try to angle my hand so her head turns towards the rabbits underneath her nose. One of them hops about. *It is just there.* She still ignores it. I don't understand. She cranes her neck to the other end of the field, again. And then my fist is empty. She's gone, flying to the far side of the field, very low, very fast, dancing about the tops of the short nettles, missing one rabbit, making split-second calculations and attention-switches, then crashing down on another. These are the rabbits she has been conversing with.

I run towards the spot. I can't see her anywhere. *Where is she?* There are nettles everywhere, but it's only regrowth, a mere three inches high. *Where is my hawk?* I hold my breath. Silence. And then I hear muffled, muffled bells. And finally I spot her head, snaking up out of the nettles. *What the–* She looks like she's broken, crushed, as if gravity had suddenly increased tenfold; her wings fanned, feathers bent upwards along their vanes from the pressure. Ah: I see now. Her wings are spread to brace herself against the ground, because she has hold of the rabbit, and the rabbit is down the hole, and she's holding on and bracing with all her might to stop herself being pulled underground. Her beak is open with the effort. I reach down the hole, feel my way along her impossibly long shins and encounter a rabbit foot. She has it, but only just. I grab the leg, and try to work out how to extract the rabbit from the hole. I pull a little, and the rabbit kicks. Goshawk squeaks. I change the angle, and slowly, like an evil, rural conjuror, pull the rabbit out of the hole, and toss it onto the grass. Mabel stamps and dances, changes her hold from hind leg to head, and the rabbit is still. She is in such a rage that she stamps up and down on the rabbit for ages, once it's dead, and then starts plucking it. She plucks for minutes and soon we are surrounded by a deep circle of soft grey fur.

The conversation of death. The sentence kept coming to mind. I'd think of it at odd moments – while taking a bath, scratching my nose, leaning to grab a mug of hot tea. My subconscious was trying to tell me something and though it was shouting very loudly indeed, I didn't hear what it was saying. Things were going wrong. Very wrong. One afternoon Mabel leapt up from her perch to my fist, lashed out with one foot and buried four talons in my bare right arm. I froze. Blood was dripping on the kitchen floor. I could do nothing. Her grip was too powerful. I had to wait until she decided to let go. The pressure was immense, but the pain, though agonising, was happening to someone else. *Why has she footed me?* I thought wildly, after she released her grip and continued as if nothing had happened at all. *She has never been aggressive before*. I was sure I'd done nothing to provoke her. Is she overkeen? Is the weighing machine broken? I spent a good quarter of an hour fussing about with piles of tuppences, trying to calibrate it. There was nothing wrong with it at all. But something was wrong with me. It wasn't just a hawk-inflicted injury. I was becoming vastly anxious. I jumped in panic when the postman knocked on the door; recoiled from the ringing phone. I stopped seeing people. Cancelled my gallery talk. Deadlocked the front door. Out on the hill I fled from walkers, dodged behind hedges when farm vehicles drove up the track. Some days I lay in bed in so much mysterious pain I began to believe the only explanation was a terminal disease.

You could explain what it was like by running to books and papers. You could read Freud, you could read Klein. You could read any number of theories about attachment and loss and grief. But those kinds of explanations come from a world the hawk wasn't in. They aren't any help. They are like explaining how it feels to be in love by waving an MRI scan of a lovestruck brain. You have to look in different places.

The anthropologist Rane Willerslev once lived for a year in a Yukaghir community in north-eastern

Siberia and became fascinated by how their hunters saw the relationship between humans and animals. The hunters, he wrote, think 'humans and animals can turn into each other by temporarily taking on one another's bodies'. If you want to hunt elk, you dress in elkskins, walk like an elk, take on an elk's alien consciousness. If you do this, elk will recognise you as one of their own and walk towards you. But, Willerslev explained, Yukaghir hunters consider these transformations very dangerous, because they can make you lose sight of your 'original species identity and undergo an invisible metamorphosis'. Turning into an animal can imperil the human soul. Willerslev included the story of a hunter who'd been tracking reindeer for many hours and ended up in an unfamiliar camp, where women he did not know gave him lichen to eat and he started forgetting things. He remembered his wife but could not remember her name. Confused, he fell asleep, and it was only when he dreamed he was surrounded by reindeer urging him to leave that he saw what he had done.

That story made me shiver when I read it, because that was what it was like. I'd turned myself into a hawk – taken all the traits of goshawks in the books and made them my own. I was nervous, highly strung, paranoid, prone to fits of terror and rage; I ate greedily or didn't eat at all; I fled from society, hid from everything; found myself drifting into strange states where I wasn't certain who or what I was. In hunting with Mabel, day after day, I had assumed – in my imagination, of course, but that was all it could ever be – her alien perspective, her inhuman understanding of the world. It brought something akin to madness, and I did not understand what I had done. When I was small I'd thought turning into a hawk would be a magical thing. What I'd read in *The Sword in the Stone* encouraged me to think it, too, as a good and instructive thing; a lesson in life for the child who would be king. But now the lesson was killing me. It was not at all the same.

Two days before the service something very strange happened on the hill. We'd been walking up a hedgerow running down the edge of a field of undersown stubble. There was a pheasant in the hedge; I'd heard it cluck and run, rat-wise, along the damp and nettly ditch, and Mabel had heard it too. She'd crashed over the hedge and perched out of sight at the top, facing away from me. Her blood was up and mine too. I shouldered my way into the hedge, knowing that any second now the pheasant would rocket out in front of me in a burnished clatter of feathers. I pushed my head through the hedge. Heard a whoosh of air and felt a staggering blow. I reeled. Coshed by a goshawk! First only blackness, then a field of stars. Then a weird proprioceptive sense that I was wearing a crown of thorns; a complicated halo of pain around my head. She'd bounced off me, left eight talon incisions behind, and was back at the top of the tree, craning to see the pheasant, which had done what all pheasants do best: escape. I shook my head dully. *She thought I was the pheasant. She didn't know it was me.* A strange buzzing in my ears, and then a muffled calm as the endorphins kicked in. I held my hand out and whistled her down to my fist, then mechanically started working the rest of the hedge-line. We were walking into the sun at this point, and I started taking a warm, distinct pleasure in the fuzzy gold aura that bathed us. Light-headed, slightly unsure of my footing, I finally wondered, *Why is my vision strange, and why do my eyes sting?* Then, *Why is the goshawk bating at my face?*

It took me a while to work out why both. I rubbed my eyes and my hand came away soaked, dramatically and Shakespearianly, in blood. I pulled off my glasses. They were covered in it. Blood was running in streams down my forehead, into my left eye, and was now attracting the attention of a hungry goshawk.

Christ, I thought, *this is a bit Edgar Allan Poe.*

I used my sleeve and some wet grass to get the worst off. Luckily this was sufficient to make the goshawk uninterested in eating me. I felt for the talon incision: a half-inch long, deep slash right between

my eyes. Ah, yes, the sixth chakra, the seat of con-
cealed wisdom, now rouged with an austringer's
bindi. I pressed the place hard with my fingers until
it stopped bleeding.

And then I kept on hawking, stumbling across the
fields in a haze of pained euphoria. The sun had
descended behind sheets of c15tereal stratus to
become a luminous disc glowing through talc-filled
air, and it was exactly the same colour as Mabel's eye.
I held her up, comparing sun with goshawk eye and
marvelled at their correspondence. By the time we'd
reached the top of the hill my legs rebelled. *Enough*,
they said. *Enough walking. Sit down. Have a nap.*

So I sat in the stubble, woozily glorying at the
beauty of it all. The mist rising in the hollows. Flocks
of golden plover pouring over in sheaves. The way
the bluish new rapeseed leaves contrasted with the
vertical straw of the stubble at my feet. The glow of
the lost sun beneath the ridge. Crickets beginning to
sing. Rooks on their way to roost passing over us in
moving constellations of small black stars. And perhaps that cosh to the head had knocked some human
sense back into me, because when I got home I sat on
the sofa and wrote my father's eulogy, straight out,
in twenty minutes, with a small round plaster stuck
on my injured forehead.

8 Memorial

I SAT ON the train clutching the folder with the speech inside, ankles burning from the heater on the floor. Outside, winter breathed in. Papery skies. Glittering trees. A wash of backlit fields that folded and shrank as the city grew. Then I was at the church, folder in hand, staring at hundreds of feet on the black and white floor, hundreds of shoulders and ties and points of collars, hems of skirts, clicks and echoes of tiny black heels. I worried I hadn't dressed smartly enough. I was wearing a black cotton dress from Debenhams. Maybe it was the wrong thing? Why hadn't I gone and bought a *proper* outfit? Something expensive, and smart, and sharp around the edges? It took a few seconds before it struck me that my panic might not be about clothes at all. I sat down in the stalls between my mother and my brother, took their hands, light-headed with love and sorrow.

My aunt was here, my brother's partner and her parents too. We were a family. We were. I looked around for the other speakers: Ron Morgans and Alastair Campbell, who'd worked with Dad for years, and Jeremy Selwyn, another photographer, biting his lip and watching the crowds pour in.

I walked up to the lectern with the paper in my hand. I had given so many lectures, so many talks, that I'd thought this would be easy. But it was not. I was terrified. I grabbed the lectern's wooden edges to stop me from swaying. *How can I do this? Don't look at the audience*, said a voice inside me. *Pretend they're not there.*

And then another voice inside said: *Look at the audience.*

I looked. Hundreds of faces. Dad's colleagues, Dad's friends. The fear vanished in an instant. I couldn't be scared any more. And I started speaking. I told them about my father. I told them a little about his early life. I told them he had been a wonderful father. I reminded them, too, of his ridiculous inability to wear anything other than a suit – although he did make concessions on holiday, and occasionally removed his tie. I told them that on our trip to Cornwall to photograph the total eclipse we'd been standing on the beach before the skies darkened when a man who said he was the reincarnation of

King Arthur, a man wearing a silver diadem and long white robes, came up to Dad, and said, bewildered, *Why are you wearing that suit?*

Well, said Dad. *You never know who you're going to meet.*

And then I told the story I hoped they would understand.

He's a boy, standing by a fence and staring up at the sky. He's at an aerodrome, Biggin Hill, spotting RAF planes. He is nine? Ten? He's been photographing each aircraft that takes off or lands with the Box Brownie camera that hangs on a string around his neck, and putting their numbers down in a spiral-bound notebook. It is getting late. He ought to leave. Then he hears a sound he cannot place, an unfamiliar engine note, and yes, *there*, this is it, this is the moment he has dreamed of. He stares into the sky. He sees the landing lights of . . . he doesn't know what it is. *He doesn't know what it is.* It is not in any of the books. He takes its picture. He copies its registration number onto the page. It is a visitation from the future: a new American Air Force plane. To the boy plane-spotter of the 1950s, it is like seeing the Holy Grail.

When I was writing the speech, still a little concussed, I reached for the phone to call my father and

ask what type of plane it was, and for a moment the
world went very black.

A hand fell on his shoulder, and a voice said,
'Come with me, laddie.' They frogmarched him to
the guardhouse, pushed him through the door, and
there, behind a desk, a sergeant-major type with a
moustache and a frown stood up, barked at him,
ripped the page out of his notebook, screwed it into
a ball and threw it in the bin, shouted some more,
took the back off the camera, exposed the roll of
film, pulled it out in loops of falling acetate and
dumped that in the bin too. *I was crying my eyes out*,
Dad said. *They said, 'Go home. You didn't see anything.
Forget you were here.' And they dumped me back at the
perimeter and I stood there with my notebook and the
Brownie, sobbing away. But then I stopped crying,
because I'd thought of something. Something out of* Dick
Barton *or the* Eagle. *Maybe I'd written hard enough.*
Using his pencil, he shaded the page of his notebook
with graphite, and there, white on grey, impressed
on the paper from the missing page above, was the
registration number of the secret plane. He stopped
crying, he said, and cycled home in triumph.

I sat down, dazed. Sun through windows. Things,
one after another. The achingly beautiful singing of
the choir. The canon's prayers. Eulogies praising my

father's photographic skills. When Alastair Campbell walked to the lectern he read Wordsworth's 'Composed upon Westminster Bridge' and prefaced it with a short speech in which he said, with decided emphasis, that my father was a Good Man. This broke me. I hadn't expected this. Or not *this* much this. Everyone sang 'Jerusalem' and I forced my mouth to move, but nothing came out but whispered fragments. And afterwards, out in the shaded churchyard under the trees, a young guy with misted glasses and a purple knitted cardigan walked up, shying nervously, and said, 'You don't know me. I don't know anyone in there. They're all the big guns. But I wanted to say that . . . well. I'm a photographer now. I'm making a living out of it. I moved to London to try and make it, and I didn't know what I was doing. And I met your dad out on a job once and he talked to me. He gave me lots of advice. He helped me. He didn't have to, but he did. He saved my life. He was amazing . . .' And he tailed off, and looked embarrassed, and I stepped forward and gave him a hug, because I didn't know what to say. And more and more people came up and talked about Dad; and all the old guard were there, snappers from back in the 1960s, and I finally got to put names to the bylines I'd seen so many times. They told me they liked the story. They said it was nice to know that my father was a born journalist. That the boy in short trousers was already the man they'd known, the man who had always got the picture, had always pulled the story from the jaws of defeat.

Down in the Press Club after the service the drinks were poured. And poured. And poured some more. Everyone became increasingly expansive, rushed up to tell me stories about my father. The stories got more slurred as the drinking went on, and the hugs and cheek-kisses increasingly off-target. 'Another drink?' said one pressman. 'Just a soft drink,' I said, and back he came with a vast glass of wine. 'Um, is there any soft drink?' I said, embarrassed. He frowned. 'That's what I brought you. This is a soft drink.'

I left with a song in my heart. I felt my family had expanded by about two hundred people, and everything was going to be fine. *Bless you, Dad*, I thought. *I always thought you were a legend, and it turns out you really, really were.*

All the way home on the train I thought of Dad and the terrible mistake I had made. I'd thought that to heal my great hurt, I should flee to the wild. It was what people did. The nature books I'd read told me so. So many of them had been quests inspired by grief or sadness. Some had fixed themselves to the stars of elusive animals. Some sought snow geese. Others snow leopards. Others cleaved to the earth, walked trails, mountains, coasts and glens. Some sought wildness at a distance, others closer to home. 'Nature in her green, tranquil woods heals and soothes all afflictions,' wrote John Muir. 'Earth hath no sorrows that earth cannot heal.'

Now I knew this for what it was: a beguiling but dangerous lie. I was furious with myself and my own unconscious certainty that this was the cure I needed. Hands are for other human hands to hold. They should not be reserved exclusively as perches for hawks. And the wild is not a panacea for the human soul; too much in the air can corrode it to nothing.

And by the time I got home I'd worked out, too, why Mabel had been behaving so strangely. She'd grown heavy with muscle over our weeks on the hill, and though she was flying at a higher weight than before, over this last week she'd got too low. She was *hungry*. Hunger had made her aggressive.

I was furious with myself when I realised that first great error on the train. But this second realisation brought self-hatred. I'd been so blind, so miserable, I'd not seen my hawk was miserable too. I'd not seen her at all. I remembered the man I'd fallen for after my father died. I'd hardly known him, but it didn't matter. I'd recruited him to serve my loss, made him everything I needed. No wonder he had run away. And now I'd made the same mistake again. I'd fled to become a hawk, but in my misery all I had done was turn the hawk into a mirror of me.

The next evening, weak with relief and the sense that something huge, something tectonic, had shifted in my world, I gave Mabel a whole dead pigeon to eat in the grey, cool evening. We sat on a chair under the apple tree, listening to blackbirds chinking in the hedge. The house didn't seem unfriendly any more. The kitchen window threw a soft square of light into the garden. Huge frosty piles of pigeon feathers accumulated on the lawn. And then she ate. Every last scrap. When it was finished her crop was so full she could hardly stand.

With the plucking of the pigeon came more revelations, as if with its uncovering other things were uncovered. I thought of the dreams I'd had that spring of the hawk slipping away into air. I'd wanted to follow it, fly with it, and disappear. I had thought for a long while that I was the hawk – one of those sulky goshawks able to vanish into another world, sitting high in the winter trees. But I was not the hawk, no matter how much I pared myself away, no matter how many times I lost myself in blood and leaves and fields. I was the figure standing underneath the tree at nightfall, collar upturned against the damp, waiting patiently for the hawk to return.

Melanie Klein wrote that children go through states of mind comparable to mourning, and that this early mourning is revived whenever grief is experienced in later life. She thought that adults try to manage newer losses the way they managed older ones. I thought of that drawing of a kestrel, its carefully worked jesses pencilled over and over again by my six-year-old hand with all its desperate insistence on the safety of knots and lines.

Some part of me that didn't work according to the everyday rules of the world but with the logic of myths and dreams had hoped that somewhere in another world was my father. His death had been so sudden. There had been no time to prepare for it, no sense in it happening at all. He could only be lost. He was out there, still, somewhere out there in that tangled wood with all the rest of the lost and dead. I know now what those dreams in spring had meant, the ones of a hawk slipping through a rent in the air into another world. I'd wanted to fly with the hawk to find my father; find him and bring him home.

9 Magical places

LAST NIGHT THE forecast was bad. A storm surge threatened to inundate East Anglia. All night I kept waking, listening to the rain, fearing for the caravans along the coast, their frail silver backs against the rain and rising seas. But the storm surge held back at the brink, and the morning dawned blue and shiny as a puddle.

After lunch I take Mabel up to the hill. Fractious gusts of wind rattle the hedgerows, blowing voluminous shoals of leaves over us as we walk up the track. There's sticky mud, and pheasant prints in it. Flocks of fieldfares *chak chak* and dodge in the hawthorns by the cow field, breaking low when we get too near, bouncing over the hedge and away in thrushy strobes of black and white. It's nice to see them. Proper winter is here. And Mabel is fizzing with happiness, wagging her tail in barely suppressed excitement, tummy feathers fluffed over her grippy toes, eyes gleaming silver in the sun. If this hawk could speak, she'd be singing under her breath. Something has changed inside me. Today it's hard to slip into the exquisite, wordless sharpness of being a hawk. Or rather, the hawk seems more human today. A rabbit lopes across the path twenty yards away and she chases it; swings up into a poplar, clutching onto a thin, near-vertical branch and leaning into the wind, narrow as a stoat. She looks about. Sees something. Goes to the next tree, looks down. Then flies back to the first one. I proffer my fist. She comes down immediately, and off we go again. *Raah*, she says. *More*.

By the hayrolls we sneak through the side of the wood, and then make our way to the corner of the top field. I'm a little blurry. I've combated the tiredness with two double espressos at breakfast and a caffeinated soda after lunch. Mabel clocks a pile of woodpigeons on plough a quarter of a mile away and makes as if to bate at them. 'Don't be daft, Mabes,' I say, but she bates anyway. *Pah*. She looks me directly in the face. *Give me something to chase!*

I do. We walk through chest-high thistles at the corner of the next field, hawk held high as I negotiate the thorns. She's gripping hard with all eight talons, bracing herself against the oncoming gusts of wind. And then out of nowhere, coming out of the ground right from where the tip of my shadow ends, a cock pheasant in bronze and bottle green, all rackety tail and sharp primaries, clatters up from the dry grass, gos already close behind. He turns downwind. She's gaining on him. No more than six inches behind the tip of his tail. But she hasn't flown much in winds like this, and mistimes her attack; is pushed by the wind a little askew, and the pheasant pulls away, climbs up over the wood. She follows, and both are lost to view. I'm just about to start running, but she's already on her way back to me, coming in at treetop height over the wood like a Mustang in a war movie. One vast, stylish arc, carving right through the barricade of oncoming air, like, *Here I come!*, and she's back on the fist, grinning like an idiot, and her whole attitude is, like, *Well! What did you think of that?*

As the days drive deeper into winter, a small and fugitive gleam begins to touch the edges of things. It happens without much fuss. I catch myself watching the sky in the morning and liking simply how it looks. Gone is the austringer's calculating eye, concerned only with wind-speed, bearing, likely precipitation. I call on old friends, make plans for the future. I look for a house to rent. My mother comes to visit.

The American writer and ecologist Aldo Leopold once wrote that falconry was a balancing act between wild and tame – not just in the hawk, but inside the heart and mind of the falconer. That is why he considered it the perfect hobby. I am starting to see the balance is righting, now, and the distance between Mabel and me increasing. I see, too, that her world and my world are not the same, and some part of me is amazed that I ever thought they were.

Then I find myself doing something surprising. I raise Mabel's weight even more and let her range more widely when she flies. This is terrible falconry. 'Never let a goshawk self-hunt,' say the books. 'Such independence is the fastest way to lose your hawk.' I know I shouldn't slip her unless there's quarry, right there, in front of her. But how can I resist this method of hawking? Today I walked up to the crest of a hill on a freezing, smoky afternoon, the whole Cambridgeshire countryside laid out in front in woods and fields and copses beneath us, all bosky and bright with golden sunshine, and I can see that what Mabel wants to do is launch a prospecting attack on the hedgerow over the rise. I let her go. Her tactical sense is magnificent. She drops from the fist, and sets off, no higher than a hand's width above the ground, using every inch of the undulating relief as cover, gathering speed until the frosty stubble winks and flashes under her, and she curves over the top of the hill. Then she sets her wings and glides, using gravity and momentum to race downhill, flash up over the top of the hedge in a sudden flowering of cream and white, a good hundred yards away, and then continue down the hedge's far side, invisible to me. I'm running, all this time, my feet caked with mud, feeling earthbound but transported at the same time.

I find her in the hedge bottom, holding onto a rabbit. 'Mabel,' I say, 'you are behaving like a wild hawk. Shocking.' This is nerve-racking falconry, but a wonderful thing. I am testing the lines between us that the old falconers would have called love. They have not broken; they do not look likely to break. Maybe they will. I raise her weight even more, and slowly the world widens. But I'm pushing my luck, and I know it.

She's not in condition, I tell myself all the way there in the car. *You'll lose her.* It is two days later, and I can hear the voice of reason telling me to go back home. I keep driving. Rain spots the windscreen and spines the nearside windows. Will the rabbits be lying out, in this weather? Maybe. I park on the muddy verge against the wet fence at the far side of the field. She's not in yarak, but she's looking about. *Whatever*, I think; I change her jesses and let her go. She chases a rabbit to its hole and swings up into an oak tree. I whistle. She doesn't seem to hear me. The rain starts falling in earnest. At this point, I realise something has changed about the space between the goshawk and me. Usually it's taut with attention. When she flies into a tree all my attention is turned to the hawk, and the hawk turns all her attention to me. Not any more. She ignores me.

There is something religious about the activity of looking up at a hawk in a tall tree. Sir Thomas Sherley wrote in the seventeenth century that flying falcons turns one's eyes to the heavens, which is why falconry is a moral activity. This seems more akin to falling to my knees begging redemption from an indifferent deity. Mabel flies on, deeper into the trees. I follow her. She's still ignoring me. *Look at me, hawk,* I'm willing up at the treetops – and she doesn't. I find myself on someone's lawn; I've trailed dark footfalls across the blue grass. The hawk is thirty feet above me and I'm shouting and whistling like a madwoman. Rain blows everywhere. I caper about. I chuck chick corpses high in the air. They fall with a thump to the grass and she doesn't even turn her head to track their sad parabolae. I whistle some more. Wave my arms. 'Mabel!' I shout. 'Come on!'

A sash window grates – an upstairs window of the huge Georgian house I've been pretending isn't there. A maid leans out. Black dress, white pinafore, white hat. Nothing about this strikes me as strange. I have followed my hawk and walked backwards in time. It's 1923. Any minute now Poirot will wander towards me across the lawn. Only later do I realise I had probably interrupted some erotic afternoon adventure.

'Are you all right?' she calls.

'I'm really sorry!' I shout back. 'I've lost my hawk.'

I point vaguely up at the tree. 'I'm trying to get her back. I'm *so* sorry to trespass on your lawn; I'll be gone soon. Just desperate to get her back.'

'Oh?'

She thinks about it for a second, looks up at the tree. Then she looks down at me. 'That's . . . fine,' she says. 'I only wanted to see if you were all right.' She slams the window. The window slams *hard*, and the hawk moves. She flies from tree to tree, taking me away from the lawn towards the edge of the wood. The trees here are taller: now my hawk is the size of a thumbnail. Light shines dully from her spangled front. And out of nowhere, her half-size copy, a miniature doppelgänger, appears. The female sparrowhawk stoops at her, turns, and stoops again. It's like Peter Pan being mobbed by his own shadow. My hawk flies to the next tree. By now I've no discernible thoughts. I know she won't come down. I must just follow her, stumbling through bushes in a quixotic delirium.

Snowberries, I think, as the white nubs brush against my hawking waistcoat. *Didn't Victorian game-keepers plant them as cover for pheasants? Oh. Oh no.* As soon as the thought is made, I see her twist out of the treetop, swerve to avoid a branch, and then stoop at a fifty-degree angle, wings almost entirely closed. It's exciting enough to make me hold my breath, but I haven't time: I'm already running. I duck under an electric fence, and my heart sinks. She's stooped into a city of pheasants. They are *everywhere. We shouldn't be here. We shouldn't be here.* I can hear her bell ringing. Where is she? Over the muddy ditch, and I'm in the wood. It is silent with leaves and fear. Then I hear pheasants running. I see one, two, three crouching in mortal terror. And then a blue-rumped cock pheasant burning copper against the leaves kicked up behind him, running hell for leather along the ground thirty feet away. Mabel comes up behind him like a gust of wind carrying the angel of death. I can't stop this. Nothing can. She's moving faster than seems plausible, powering down on a glide-slope that ends abruptly: she binds to the pheasant with both feet just as he sticks his head into a pile of brushwood. And then all hell breaks loose. Leaves fly, feathers fly, pheasant wings batter, and I'm running.

I'm nearly passing out with stress, crouching, dirty, covered in mud and sweat, pulsing with adrenalin. The goshawk is full of adrenalin too. She's killing the pheasant more, even though it's dead. *Stamp stamp, gripe, stamp, foot, clutch, stamp.* Leaves continue to fly as she dances about on it. Her eyes burn with an unholy light, her beak is open. She looks terrifying. Slowly she calms down. I keep looking back behind me. No one is in sight. I feed her all the food in my waistcoat, and give her the whole head and neck of the pheasant. I sneak the pheasant

itself into the capacious back pocket of the waistcoat, breaking its long tail feathers in half so no
tell-tale ends poke out of the zip, and guiltily heap
leaves all over the scene of the crime. And then we
sneak back to the car.

I am undone. From the four corners of the field I'm
crossing, from all sides, every single cock pheasant in
the neighbourhood begins to crow simultaneously.
It's a terrible, echoing, barrelling sound, like an echo-
effects pedal on long sustain, rolling backwards and
forwards through the air. It swells into the most terrifying, sustained cacophony, more like an artillery
bombardment than calling birds. It is a vast alarum
of accusation. I am guilty. I've poached a pheasant
from someone's shoot. *I didn't mean to,* I almost say
out loud. *It was an accident.* I'm relieved when the
calls die away. And then, as I round the corner to the
car, the barrage starts again. Chastened and slightly
unnerved, I drive away, the pheasants gone but con-
science ringing in my ears.

The landscape is changing before my eyes. What I
see is not just winter moving onwards to spring; it
is a land filling slowly with spots and lines of beauty.
There's brittle sun out on the hill this lunchtime, and
a fresh westerly wind. Mabel's pupils shrink to opi-
ated pinpricks as I unhood her, both of her eyes
narrow with happiness. It is exceptionally clear. The

red flag over the range cracks with the wind and the sound of distant rifles; the radio mast on the horizon looks like an ink-drawing over a wash of shadows and lines and bolts of land rippling up to the chalk hills before me. We walk up the track. From the top I can look down and see the whole of Cambridge. The light today is beguiling. The rooftops and spires seem within a hand's grasp; a chess-set town glittering among bare trees, as if I could pick up the brute tower of the university library and move it six places north, set it down somewhere else.

From here, the city is mild and small, and looks all of a piece with the landscape around it. The beauty of a vantage like this is that it obscures the roads and walls with trees, makes Cambridge a miniature playset of forest-set blocks and spires. These days, when I go into town, I'm increasingly finding excuses to park my car in the multi-storey car park, because from the open-air fourth floor I can stare at these fields. They run like a backbone across the horizon, scratched with copse-lines and damped with cloud-shadow. A strange complication arises when I look at them. Something of a doubling. Leaning out over the car-park rail, I feel myself standing on the distant hill. There's a terrible strength to this intuition. It's almost as if my soul really is up there, several miles away, standing on thistly clay watching my soul-less self standing in the car park, with diesel and concrete in her nose and anti-skid asphalt under her feet. With the car-park self thinking if she looked very, very hard, perhaps through binoculars, she might see herself up there.

I feel I might be up there, because now the hill is home. I know it intimately. Every hedgerow, every track through dry grass where the hares cut across field-boundaries, each discarded piece of rusted machinery, every earth and warren and tree. By the road, half an acre of fenced-off mud, scaled with tyre-tracks and water reflecting pieces of sky. Wagtails, pallets, tractors, a broken silo on its side like a fallen rocket stage. Here is the sheep-field, there is the clover ley, now mown and turned to earth. Further up the track are tracts of mugwort: dead now from frost, seeds clinging to stems and branches like a billion musty beads on ragged Christmas trees. Piles of bricks and rubble run along the left-hand side of the track, and the earth between them is soft and full of rabbits. Further up the hill the hedges are higher, and by the time I get to the top the track has narrowed into grass. Cow parsley. Knapweed. Wild burdock. The argillaceous shimmer of tinder-fine clay. Drifts of chalk beneath. Yellowhammers chipping in the hedges. Cumulus rubble. The maritime light of this island, set as it is under a sky mirrored and uplit by sea.

I don't own this land. I've only got permission to

fly here. But in walking it over and over again and paying it the greatest attention I've made it mine. I know where its animals live, and how they move about it. Know that the larks sleep on the top of the hill, but on sunny mornings they move to warm themselves on eastward slopes. That when the weather is wet but the rain has stopped, the rabbits in the warrens near the ditches move eastward onto the drier fields to graze. This sense of where the animals are is the coincidence of long experience with unconsciously noted clues. The incidence of sunlight on a stubblefield, and the pressure of wind on the same. The precise colour of the ground. I move towards the larks as if I could see them.

But the biggest field – one planted with oilseed rape – is not like the others. It is a mystery. Walking it with Mabel is like playing natural-historical battleships. Anything could be living in those thick-packed bluish leaves. Pheasants, partridges, hares – even a jack snipe, whirring up with snappy wingbeats from a muddy patch near the hedge. It seems ludicrous that anything could be invisible in a bare two inches of herbage. But everything is. There is a sense of creation about it: when the hare leapt up from our feet today it was as if it had been made by the field *ex nihilo*. The hare had an ally: a strong north-easterly. Mabel tried twice to grab it, and both times it jinked across the wind and she missed. It is very strange watching a hawk chase a land animal in a high wind. The hare has purchase: its claws and furry pads dig into leaves and mud, and it uses the ground to propel itself against. But the hawk moves in air alone. It is like watching one element against another. One world versus another, like a gannet diving into the sea for fish. I am glad she did not catch the hare.

There is the tree Mabel dived from to cosh me on the head. There's the invisible line in the air along which for the very first time she followed a cock pheasant to cover. There's the hedge where she clung, tail fanned wide, wings pressed against twigs, looking for a pigeon already gone. There is the bramble bush that tripped me and pitched me into a flooded ditch. The hawk and I have a shared history of these fields. There are ghosts here, but they are not long-dead falconers. They are ghosts of things that happened.

It's a child's world, full of separate places. Give me a paper and pencil now and ask me to draw a map of the fields I roamed about when I was small, and I cannot do it. But change the question, and ask me to list what was there and I can fill pages. The wood ants' nest. The newt pond. The oak covered in marble galls. The birches by the motorway fence with fly agarics at their feet. These things were the waypoints of my world. And other places became magic through happenstance. When I found a huge red underwing moth behind the electricity junction box at the end of my road, that box became a magic place. I needed to check behind it every time I walked past, though nothing was ever there. I'd run to check the place where once I'd caught a grass snake, look up at the tree that one afternoon had held a roosting owl. These places had a magical importance, a pull on me that other places did not, however devoid of life they were in all the visits since.

And now I'm giving Mabel her head, and letting her fly where she wants, I've discovered something rather wonderful. She is building a landscape of magical places too. She makes detours to check particular spots in case the rabbit or the pheasant that was there last week might be there again. It is wild superstition, it is an instinctive heuristic of the hunting mind, and it works. She is learning a particular way of navigating the world, and her map is coincident with mine. Memory and love and magic. What happened over the years of my expeditions as a child was a slow transformation of my landscape over time into what naturalists call a local patch, glowing with memory and meaning. Mabel is doing the same. She is making the hill her own. Mine. Ours.

10 The new world

IT IS CHRISTMAS Eve. Outside my window is an icy tidal river. Everything not fringed with silver and limned lamp-black is white or Prussian blue. Those moving dots are wintering ducks and a loon slides past them on a low, submarine-profile cruise to the sea. Everything is heavy with snow. I'm stuffed to the gills with pancakes and maple bacon and I'm feeling quiet inside, quieter now than at any time since my father died. It is a deep and simple hush. My mother is asleep in the room next door, my brother is home with his in-laws, and Mabel is at Stuart and Mandy's, three thousand miles away.

Mum and I are spending Christmas in America through the kindness of my friend Erin and his parents Harriet and Jim, who run a bed-and-breakfast inn on the coast of southern Maine. I met Erin years ago when I worked breeding falcons in Wales; a young surfer and falconer, he'd turned up at Carmarthen station looking wildly out of place, like a clean-shaven Cary Elwes in *The Princess Bride*. He'd been drawn to Britain by dreams of flying falcons, only to be put to work jetwashing aviaries in driving rain. But he survived the gloom, and we became friends. Proper friends. The kind people say you only make once, twice in a life. I've visited him many times over the years, and through him I've met a crowd of wonderful Mainers. They're not much like my Cambridge friends. They're fishermen, hunters, artisans, teachers, innkeepers, guides. They make furniture, decoys, exquisite ceramic pots. They cook, they teach, they fish for lobster, take tourists out to catch striped bass. And most of them hunt.

Hunting in Maine is not obviously riven with centuries of class and privilege. There are no vast pheasant shoots here where bankers vie for the largest bags, no elite grouse moors or exclusive salmon rivers. All the land can be hunted over by virtue of common law, and locals are very proud of this egalitarian tradition. Years ago I read an article in a 1942 edition of *Outdoor Life* that stirred wartime sentiment by appealing to it. 'One of my grandfathers came from northern Europe for the single reason that he wanted to live in a country where he could try to catch a fish without sneaking onto some nobleman's property where the common people were excluded,' one hunter explained. In fascist Italy and

Germany, the article went on, hunting is limited to 'the owners of estates, their guests, and the high and mighty'. It had to back-pedal slightly, of course, for the same was true in Britain. 'This is no slap at our courageous ally,' it explained. 'But we do not need her system of land management.' What's more, hunting is far more acceptable here than it is in Britain. One of my friends in Maine is Scott McNeff, a wiry and energetic firebrand who runs an ice-cream emporium in summer and spends the winter flying his hawks. He told me that few households in the whole state aren't touched by the November deer hunt. Even if people don't hunt deer themselves, everyone knows someone who does, and freezers across Maine are full of home-shot venison packaged and parcelled out for friends and families. People swap hunting stories here the way people swap drinking stories at home.

Scott took us hawking yesterday with his male redtailed hawk, a first-year bird called Yoder. He's a handsome beast: his crown and back are chestnut brown, his underparts milk-glass white, sparsely marked with a gorget of spots and dashes. He's not as well-armed as a gos; his toes are shorter, thicker, more like fists than Mabel's armoured pianist's fingers. He has nothing of a goshawk's rangy, leopard-like hunch or contagious apprehension. His eyes are dark, his face mild and open. A thick-set, amiable hawk. An unflappable kind of hawk. And he has been borrowed from the wild. Yoder is a passage hawk, one who already knows how to hunt, who has in the weeks since leaving his nest had to learn a hundred different ways of encountering air and rain and wind and quarry, and learn them fast to survive. American falconers are permitted to trap and fly a bird like this over its first winter, and then release it in the spring to return to the wild and breed. Falconers here can do this because they are tested and licensed by the state. It's a good system. I wish we had it at home.

Scott has the kind of fluid physicality that makes everything he does beautiful to watch. He changes the hawk's jesses, checks there's food in the pocket of his battered jacket, and we set out. The ground has a deep crust of snow. Everything is poised as if it might shake itself. There are woods here: thousands upon thousands of acres of white pine, of hemlock, spruce and oak. But that is not where we are going. We walk across what looks like a school playground. Yoder leaves Scott's fist, flies up onto a children's playframe. We clamber down a slope behind timber-lapped houses. The hawk follows. The air swallows sound, so that speaking into it your voice stops a foot in front of your face in a cloud of white breath. *What are we doing here?* I think dully. *This is a town.*

Skittering flakes of dislodged bark fall through thirty feet of air. A family waves from an upstairs window. We wave back. The hawk is laddering up a pine tree behind their backyard fence, hoisting itself skyward with leaps and hawkish flourishes. 'Squirrel!' shouts Scott, and I am knee-deep in snow, coughing, my jetlagged ears singing in the hush, attempting to follow what is happening above me. The brightness above is blank behind knots and spars of twigs and needles. The flight is the workings out of two creatures above me. Height, vantage, escape, evasion. The squirrel knows about redtails. They live in these woods. The redtail knows about squirrels, too, has hunted them in the wild before Scott trapped him earlier that fall. A thin branch bends and springs back as the squirrel leaps into the next tree, the hawk after it. We crane our necks up at the war above, playing out like a wildscreen *The Enemy Below*. The hawk twists, the squirrel makes another leap, is silhouetted black against the sky, legs outstretched, and then a blunt, black form hits it. It is the hawk. I hear the impact, see the awkward, parachuting fall through thirty feet of snowy, splintered air and they land heavily on the ground, and Scott is running in slow motion through deep snow, and when I get there the squirrel is dead, and the hawk is mantling over his prey, wings out, beak open. A thin stream of smoke climbs from his mouth. Blood has already melted a thin line through the snow and the hawk's feet and feathers are powdered with a crumbly paste of snow and blood that resembles decorative sugar. The hawk looks up and about at his surroundings. A back yard, garages, a low fence. A barbecue heaped deep with snow. An inflatable Santa riding an inflatable Harley Davidson. Icicles hanging from Christmas eaves. Somewhere I can hear a television, and beyond that someone is singing 'Happy Birthday'. I have never seen anything so fiercely wild and so familiar. How can it be here? How can the wild be here in this back-lot in the middle of a town, in the midst of home and community? These are the things I had flown from.

It was the wildest hunt I had ever seen. Sitting by the window staring out at the sliding river, I begin to wonder if home can be anywhere, just as the wild can be at its fiercest in a run of suburban back-lots, and a hawk might find a lookout perch on a children's play-frame more useful than one on the remotest pine. Maine has given me a family for Christmas and shown me a hawk can be part of it too. It's shown me that you can reconcile the wild. You can bring it home with you.

It's our last morning. Erin, Mum and I are walking along Parsons Beach, bracing ourselves against the wind. It is a bitter, salt cold day; we tread on frozen sand. Strings of seaducks fly far offshore, ragged lines over soaked slate baize. The waters under them are full of lobsters; Maine is famous for them; signs for lobster rolls hang everywhere across town. Erin's dad had been a lobsterman once, and I'd gone out fishing with them years ago. Which is to say, I sat on the deck of their boat and watched as they hauled traps, measured, sorted and banded lobsters, rebaited the traps and set them overboard. They worked for hours while I sat there, unable to help, unable to do anything except watch. They were delighted I'd come out with them, and it was a wonderful day, but I felt guilty all the same: I was an English tourist out of her depth. Walking on the beach I remembered that boat-trip and felt uncomfortable as hell. I'd spent months out with Mabel on the hill. I'd seen the harvest come in, tractors harrowing slopes, stockmen turning sheep out to winter in the fields. And I'd not spoken to anyone. No one at all. I thought of the summer tourists here standing in packs to photograph the lobster boats coming in, or angling their cameras to catch the twisted light and shade on stacks of lobster traps on Cape Porpoise quay. Was I like that? I hadn't meant to be a tourist with my hawk. It didn't feel like tourism. But I sure as hell had avoided being part of the working world.

We turn back, walking into the wind now, crunching over ice-crusted rockweed and sending sanderling flocks swirling along the tideline. The off-season streets are deserted, the hotels closed, shutters down, wooden signboards swinging in the wind. A Cooper's hawk sits on the overhead stop-light on the intersection of Main Street and Western Avenue, flat-headed and fluffed as Mabel, looking down on the empty town.

Back at the inn, feeling cold and horribly sober, I grab a coffee and pace about by the fire. My face is burning. I suppose it is from the wind. Mum is packing upstairs. Erin and his dad are in the kitchen. I can hear them laughing. *I don't want to go back*, I think. I had fled from community. At my father's memorial I'd remembered it existed. Now I am back in it, in the middle of a community, in the middle of a family home, and I do not want to leave. This place is fixing my broken heart. I can feel it mending, and I'm fearful of what will happen when I'm gone. I'm not sure how I will cope back in England, back in my jobless, hopeless, lonely old town.

The back door slams. Jim is heading off in the truck to his workshop. *I don't want to leave.* I sulk. I fret. I scowl at the fire, hot with self-pity. Then I hear the door open and Erin's tousled head appears round the frame. It wears a vastly conspiratorial expression. I sense a plan is brewing. And a minute later I'm helping him drag their huge Christmas tree out of the room and onto the snowy lawn, tip snaking through the rough trail it makes, branches skittering over and cutting through the crust that glitters in the sparse light. We prop it up in the deep snow as if it had grown there. I have no idea what is going on.

'OK, Macca, let's burn this!' he says.

Puzzlement.

'It's traditional. It's what we do here. In *America*.'

I don't believe him for a second.

'In England we dump them on the street, *traditionally*,' I say. 'Absolutely let's burn it.'

'I'll get the firelighter!' he yells. I can feel the madness to this, its contagious pagan glee. He runs back from the house with a squeezy plastic bottle of fire-lighting gel and in the snowy hush, fog collecting around us as the thaw turns ice to water that hangs in the warming air, he decorates the tree with gloopy green strings that drip and stick like glutinous tinsel.

'Stand back!' he commands. He strikes a match. A branch catches with a tearing scratch of flame. For a few moments this is pretty: a soft yellow light in the monochromatic gloom. But then there is an explosive, tearing waterfall of rearing flame that bursts into appalling brightness. Erin's eyebrows go up. He steps back a good few paces. And now I am laughing so much I can hardly stand. 'Jesus, Erin,' I shout. It's as if he's set light to the whole of the world: a twenty-foot pyramid of flame lighting the lawn, the house, the river, the far side of the river, sending black shadows out from trees that a moment ago were lost in darkness, and our faces are gilded with fierce, orange fire. *What the hell have we done?* The smoke mixes with the fog so that everything, everywhere is on fire. The incandescent tree, black twigs sintering, clicking, crumbling, and smoke, and Erin and I now wearing the faces of people who are going to be in serious trouble. 'I think we might be seeing the fire truck any moment now,' Erin shouts, and we're both of us children again, delighted at what we have made and fearful of disaster.

And then the fire is out. The skeleton stands in the snow, all its complexity gone. Just a thin trunk with a few charcoal branches, already damp in the steaming air. And I stare at the remains of the tree and breathe the smoke and fog from the air and Erin makes a face at me and I make one back.

'That,' he says, 'was excellent.'

It was. A ritual burn, a ceremony of strange, protective magic. Bad things had fled from that burning tree. We laugh all the way back to the house, leaving the skeleton upright in the snow. And later that day Mum and I fly back to London. I drive her home, promise to see her soon, then make my way to Cambridge, and Stuart and Mandy's house. I run to their door. I cannot wait to see my hawk. There she is, perched in their garden, fat and happy in a crowd of pointers with wagging tails. I thank Stuart for looking after her while I was gone. He stands by the patio doors, strangely drawn and tired. 'No worries,' he says. 'I've not done much with her, to be honest. I've had flu. It's been terrible. I've been in bed all Christmas. Just thrown her food.'

'Poor Stu,' Mandy says, coming towards the table with three cups of coffee and a packet of open biscuits. 'He's really been in the wars.' I look at my friends and my heart crumples. They have spent so many hours helping me, have shown me so much love. And I had taken it all for granted.

'Thank you. Thank you so much,' I say. 'I love you guys. I really do.' I say it with as much feeling as I can. I am not just thanking them for looking after my hawk. I get up to give Stuart a hug. 'Don't catch it,' he says, backing away. I hug him anyway.

11 Winter histories

THERE'S A COMPLICATED sky of cold-front ragged cloud under swathes of high cirrostratus, and a head-wind that sends larks up like chaff as we walk through the fields. Clouds of linnets bounce, half-midges, half musical notation, along the hedges surrounding my old home, and all is out of sorts as far as that notion of home lies because my father isn't here. It is late winter and I'm back at my mother's house. Things are better now, I know, and I've been coming here more often, but each time I forget how hard it will be.

The winter fields are shorn, yellowed into stalky, rabbit-grazed sward spotted with foraging rooks. I can hawk with Mabel all the way across this land until it ends in a slumpy hedge so wide it's almost a wood, furrily iced with old-man's-beard. Beyond it is someone else's land; a *terra incognita*, holding the suppressed fascination we all have for places just beyond where we know, or are supposed to be. I stand at the top of the field, change her jesses, remove her leash, thread the swivel onto it, double back the leash, and stuff it deep into my pocket. I hold my arm high, wait for her to look about, and cast her off my fist into the gusty wind. She glides down to the far hedge and swings up into a small ash, shaking her tail. I follow her down and we start hawking proper, looking for rabbits in a tangle of broken, open woodland. This line of trees is not designed for human thoroughfare. There are elder bushes, green twigs and branches starred with lichen. There are fallen oaks, clumps of vicious brambles, screens of hazel, and ivy clambering and covering stumps and extending a hand up to the trees above to scramble into the light, so the whole place is umbrous and decorated with shiny scales of ivy leaves. The air tastes of humus and decay. Each footfall breaks twigs and has that slightly uncertain, oddly hollow quality of walking on thick woodland soil.

Mabel is being extraordinary. I've mostly flown her in open country before. She has grasped how woodland hawking works, and is hugely attentive. More than attentive. Flying a goshawk in a scape of obstacles and broken sightlines makes the connection between us hugely manifest. She breaks through twigs to come down to my fist when I whistle, and she follows me as I walk, moving above me like a personal angel whenever I'm out of sight. I look up and see her crouching, staring at me with round eyes, pupils dilated with excitement and attention, crayon-yellow toes gripping dead ash branches. Or floating above me, above the branches, flickering through, sending submarine ripples behind her.

There's no narrative to be spoken of. There is the moment when I turn and see the calm, haunting face of a young rabbit looking out of a hole ten feet away, ears up, nose twitching. A little grey doe. I can't call attention to it. The world triangulates and halts dead. The rabbit and I look at each other. It realizes this stare is an involvement in death, and disappears. Mabel doesn't see it until the moment where the rabbit becomes air as it pops back down the hole, but she has to fly anyway, to the after-image, just in case; and tears off at low level and brushes the hole with one foot before swinging up high in a tree and shaking her tail, looking down. There is the moment where I'm running blindly after the hawk, and see her footing at a branch forty foot up a sweet chestnut: a failed attack at a grey squirrel, which skitters up the helically coiled saglines of the trunk and away to the safety of a high branch, and bark shards fall around me like delicate, waxen snow as Mabel returns, on call, to my fist, and I'm relieved as hell, because squirrels bite. They can take the toe off a hawk's foot. Not that I can blame them, given the circumstances. Then the moment where she comes towards me at ground level, because that's the only way through a big bank of elder twigs, and as she comes, I am watching the way the feathers on her back lift just a little as she stalls to slam into the glove – *blam* – all eight toes and talons gripping hard, then relaxing; and she looks right at me, in a blaze of expectation. And then, quite suddenly, she sees something through the trees, out there on the other side of the hedge. Her pupils grow wide. She snakes her neck and flattens her crown, and the tiny grey hair-feathers around her beak and eyes crinkle into a frown that I've learned means *there's something there.*

I decide to investigate, even though I don't have permission to fly her over there. Carefully, so as not to put it anywhere near my trousers – so far I have torn three pairs to shreds, out hawking – I high-step over the rusty fence-wire, turn about, and find myself calf-deep in dead game-cover crop the colour of wet tobacco. We are looking out across a wide downland valley. It's beautiful. I take one deep breath and exhale, full of the ballooning light-headedness of standing on chalk.

Chalk landscapes do this to me; bring an exhil-arating, on-tiptoe sense that some deep revelation is at hand. This makes me feel guilty. There's a long vein of chalk-mysticism buried in English nature-culture, and I know that what I'm feeling, standing here, partakes of it. I'm guilty because I know that loving landscapes like this involves a kind of history that concerns itself with purity, a sense of deep time and blood-belonging, and assumes that these solitudinous windswept landscapes are finer, better, than the landscapes below. 'The frequenter of downland is occupied with essentials; with structure, with forms and with textures,' wrote chalk-cult ruralist H. J. Massingham in the 1930s. 'Aloft, he breathes an air that tunes him to the grand, archaic, naked forms of things.' It's a landscape that is a parable of the aviator's eye.

I grew up in the lowland pine-forests and heaths of sandy Surrey. But there's a photograph of me, wrapped in a tartan duffel coat, laying a five-year-old hand on one of the stones at Stonehenge, where my childish brain first grasped at intimations of history. And when I was a little older, corn buntings jangling from high-ground fence posts out near Wantage, I remember my father telling me that the track we walked upon, the Ridgeway, was an ancient, ancient path. This impressed me greatly. It was the 1970s, which had seen another great burst of the cult of chalk and history: there were experimental Iron Age re-enactment villages at Butser; scary children's TV dramas about the stone circles at Avebury; great bustard reintroductions on top-secret military establishments on Salisbury Plain. Now, I wonder why. Was it some response to the oil crisis? To economic depression? I don't know. But up on the Ridgeway path, aged nine or ten, was where for the first time I realised the power a person might feel by aligning themselves to deep history. Only much later did I understand these intimations of history had their own, darker, history. That the chalk-cult rested on a presumption of organic connections to a landscape, a sense of belonging sanctified through an appeal to your own imagined lineage. That chalk downlands held their national, as well as natural, histories. And it was much later, too, that I realised these myths hurt. That they work to wipe away other cultures, other histories, other ways of loving, working and being in a landscape. How they tiptoe towards darkness.

I'm standing on the far side of my familiar hedge, looking at this *terra incognita* that is the grand twentieth-century conjuration of our mythical English past. I walk out of the cover crop to where the thin, stony soil is exposed, so thick with chalk it's like white paste; hair roots and flints, spotted with rain; tiny buttons of stone in impasto. The land falls away at my feet into a dry valley; a basin the size of a village, one beech copse hanging grey from its left-hand slope. It is a field of a million tiny tillers – little shoots of wheat. They give the chalky earth a furry tint, like algae on a cliff-face. Even in this dark, watery light, the valley shines palely. And I see what Mabel had seen. About a hundred yards in front of us, crouched in its form, is a big brown hare, black-tipped ears laid to its ginger back. But there's more, much more here: down at the bottom of the valley, where the river would be were there water, is a herd of thirty fallow deer. They are the colour of moleskin on their backs, shading to pale grey underneath. They're tight-clustered, quivering with indecision. They're watching me. Thirty upraised heads. The herd is delicate and powerful, and it is waiting to see what I will do.

I can't resist the urge that takes hold of me then. I hold on to Mabel, who is watching them too, and like a woman possessed, walk towards them, with that strange disconnect between head and feet you feel when walking downhill. I'm technically trespassing, but I can't help it. I want to interact with them in some way. I want to get closer. And as I do, the pressure of my impending arrival pushes single deer off to the right, and they walk, then canter, in a long line, along the bottom of the valley and up to the wood at the far edge of the field, a good half-mile away. They are bewitching. Mabel watches them. She is ignoring the hare. The deer in procession resemble charcoal cave paintings rendered manifest. Art's magic working backwards. The chalk behind them, bone. And now the hare runs, too. The hare runs in the opposite direction to the deer. The animals run, and the landscape seems then to be parting in front of me. Deer one way, hare the other. And now they are quite gone: the hare to the field-margin at the top of the hill to my left, the deer into the wood at the top of the hill to my right. There is nothing before me now but wind and chalk and wheat.

Nothing. The hawk rouses again and begins to preen her covert feathers. The running deer and the running hare. Legacies of trade and invasion, farming, hunting, settlement. Hares were introduced, it is thought, by the Romans. Fallow deer certainly were. Pheasants, too, brought in their burnished hordes from Asia Minor. The partridges possessing this ground were originally from France, and the ones I see here were hatched in game-farm forced-air incubators. The squirrel on the sweet chestnut? North America. Rabbits? Medieval introductions. Felt, meat, fur, feather, from all corners. But possessing the ground, all the same.

We set off, again, homeward this time. But now the rain in the air is harder, and the rabbits are so close to their holes that Mabel's not able to get a foot to them before they disappear. After one hair's-breadth miss in a rocky quarryhole by a bank of wild rose stems, I call her back and feed her up. She is tired. Beads of water spot her head and tiny eyelash feathers. We stroll back to the car park. I'm tired too, and glad to see people walking towards us. I've met them before: a retired couple from my mother's village, walking their white-muzzled terrier on a long lead. They're all wrapped up with scarves and snap-fastened country jackets and their shoulders are set a little against the cold and wet. I meet them here quite often. I've always been delighted to see them. I don't know their names, and they don't know mine, though they know my hawk's called Mabel. I wave, and they stop and wave back.

'Hello', I say.

'Hello! How's the hawk?' they ask.

'She's good,' I say happily. 'But tired. She's been flying all over the place. It's beautiful out here today. I saw the deer!' I went on, glad to have someone to tell. 'A big herd of them, dark-coated, down in the bottom of the valley.'

'Yes,' he says. 'The deer. Special, aren't they, those ones. Rare. We see them quite often.' He is smiling; we're all enjoying our shared secrets of a place. She's nodding too. 'Aren't they beautiful?' she says. 'We counted them once, didn't we?'

He nods. 'There're usually between twenty-five and thirty.'

'Thirty exactly!' I say.

'They're a lovely sight.'

I agree. She tucks her scarf more tightly around

her as a squall begins. Her husband nods vigorously, rain darkening his shoulders. 'A herd of deer,' he says, beaming, then his expression folds into something I don't recognise.

'Doesn't it gives you hope?' he says suddenly.

'Hope?'

'Yes,' he says. 'Isn't it a relief that there're things still like that, a real bit of Old England still left, despite all these immigrants coming in?'

I don't know what to say. His words hang and all the awkwardness is silence. The leaves rattle in the hazel stems. And I nod a goodbye, sad as hell, and my hawk and I trudge home through the rain.

It is a miserable walk. I should have said something. But embarrassment had stopped my tongue. Stomping along, I start pulling on the thread of darkness they'd handed me. I think of the chalk-cult countryside and all its myths of blood-belonging, and that hateful bronze falcon, of Göring's plans to exclude Jews from German forests. I think of the Finnish goshawks that made the Brecklands home, and of my grandfather, born on the Western Isles, who spoke nothing but Gaelic until he was ten. And the Lithuanian builder I'd met collecting mushrooms in a wood who asked me, bewildered, why no one he'd met in England knew which were edible, and which were not. I think of all the complicated histories that landscapes have, and how easy it is to wipe them away, put easier, safer histories in their place.

They are only safe for us. The fields where I fly Mabel back in Cambridge are farmed organically, and they are teeming with life. These are not. The big animals are here, it is true: the deer, the foxes, the rabbits; the fields look the same, and the trees, too, but look more carefully and this land is empty. There are few plants other than crops, and few bees, or butterflies, for the soil is dressed and sprayed with chemicals that kill. Ten years ago there were turtle doves on this land. Thirty years ago there were corn buntings and enormous flocks of lapwings. Seventy years ago there were red-backed shrikes, wrynecks and snipe. Two hundred years ago, ravens and black grouse. All of them are gone.

Old England is an imaginary place, a landscape built from words, woodcuts, films, paintings, picturesque engravings. It is a place imagined by people, and people do not live very long or look very hard. We are very bad at scale. The things that live in the soil are too small to care about; climate change too large to imagine. We are bad at time, too. We cannot remember what lived here before we did; we cannot love what is not. Nor can we imagine what will be different when we are dead. We live out our three score and ten, and tie our knots and lines only to ourselves. We take solace in pictures, and we wipe the hills of history.

History, and life too. It might resemble Old England here but it is not anything like the country of four hundred years ago, of one hundred years ago. I am nearly home, now, and I'm sad, and angry, and fired up as hell. I wish that we would not fight for landscapes that remind us of who we think we are. I wish we would fight, instead, for landscapes buzzing and glowing with life in all its variousness. And I am guilty too. I'd wanted to escape history by running to the hawk. Forget the darkness, forget Göring's hawks, forget death, forget all the things that had been before. But my flight was wrong. Worse than wrong. It was dangerous. *I must fight, always, against forgetting*, I thought. And I wish I had run after that couple and explained about the deer. I wish I had stood there in the mud in the rain, waving one hand with a hawk on the other, shouting about history and blood.

Later that night I find my father's plane-spotting diaries at the bottom of his bookshelves: six hardbacked, cloth-spined exercise books. I pull one out at random. 1956. He was sixteen. The pages are divided into columns, headed with careful, inked capitals: *TIME. NUMBER OF PLANES. TYPE OF PLANE. REMARKS. REGISTRATION NUMBER.* I look at the first column. On the twenty-fifth of April he starts watching at 9.40 a.m. and leaves at 7 p.m. On the twenty-sixth he starts at 9 and ends at 9 p.m. *Twelve hours of looking up at the sky. Good God.* There are hundreds of pages and thousands upon thousands of aircraft here. Vickers V70 Viscounts, F-86 Sabres, Airspeed Ambassadors, Lockheed Super Constellations, Gloster Meteors.

Here's his report of a visit to Croydon Airport at the end of May. 'Eight de Havilland Tiger Moths. Two Auster Aiglet trainers. Two Taylorcraft Plus Ds. One Auster 5. Three De Havilland 104 Doves.' I have no idea what these planes are. I find a glued-in snapshot of a Tupolev Tu 104. He has written a few lines underneath: 'This aircraft is undoubtedly a civil conversion of the Type 39 Badger but the Russians said it was a completely new aircraft.' It has all the burning pedantry I remember from my childhood obsession with hawks. Suddenly my father seems very close. Another photograph falls out. I pick it up. *De Havilland 104 Dove, Croydon Airport, 2–4–56.* I cross-check the registration number against the list. *G–AMYO. Morton Air Services.* The edge of the runway is lost in mist. I can see a tiny profile inside the cockpit, the suggestion of a man leaning forward to wipe the canopy before the plane climbs into the grey April sky.

It is then that the knowledge of why my father watched planes drops into my head. When he and his friends had been small boys running feral across London bombsites, he'd told me, they collected things. Collected anything: shrapnel, cigarette packets, coins; mostly things that came in series. Things that could be matched and swapped; sets that could be completed. Collecting things like this, I realised, must have stitched together their broken world of rubble, made sense of a world disordered by war. And my father's aeroplanes were just as much of a set to collect: a series of beautiful, moving things with names and numbers, all deeply concerned with danger and survival. But there was more. Aeroplanes had wings. They took flight, and if you knew them, watched them, understood their movements, you could somehow take flight too; you could watch that Tupolev 104 take off and know it will cross borders you cannot cross except in your imagination. In a few hours it will be on a snowy Soviet airfield. Or any one of a thousand else. In watching the planes, you fly with them and escape. They enlarge your little world and spread it across the seas.

The notebooks are full of a fierce attention to things I do not know. But now I know what they are for. These are records of ordered transcendence. A watcher's diary. My father's talk of patience had held within it all the magic that is waiting and looking up at the moving sky.

I put the notebook back and as I do I see there's a

piece of brown cardboard between the next two notebooks on the shelves. Puzzled, I pull it out. It is a blank piece of thick card cut roughly along one edge. I turn it over. My heart misses a beat, because stuck to the other side is a silver doorkey under three inches of clear tape. And five words written in pencil.

Key to flat.
Love, Dad

Dad had posted it to me last year so I could stay at his flat in London when he was away. I'd lost it, of course. 'My daughter the absent-minded professor,' he'd said, rolling his eyes. 'Don't worry. I'll get another one cut.' But he'd never got round to it, and I'd not thought of it since. I don't know what it is doing here. I read the words again and think of his hand writing them. And I think of Dad holding my own tiny hand as I put the other one flat against the sarsens at Stonehenge, back when I was very small and there were no fences to stop you walking among the stones. I looked up at the thing that was like a door but had no walls behind it.

'Is it a house, Daddy?' I asked him.

'No one knows,' he said. 'It's very, very old.'

I held the cardboard and felt its scissor-cut edge. And for the first time I understood the shape of my grief. I could feel exactly how big it was. It was the strangest feeling, like holding something the size of a mountain in my arms. *You have to be patient*, he had said. If you want to see something very much, you just have to be patient and wait. There was no patience in my waiting, but time had passed all the same, and worked its careful magic. And now, holding the card in my hands and feeling its edges, all the grief had turned into something different. It was simply love. I tucked the card back into the bookshelf. 'Love you too, Dad,' I whispered.

© Marzena Pogorzaly 2014

HELEN MACDONALD grew up in Surrey, a place she credits with indelibly shaping her writing life: 'after the stresses of school, I'd spend hours wandering its sandy paths, learning the seasonal shifts in the sounds of woodland and field. I filled diaries with sightings: moths and foxes, slow-worms, grass snakes, nightjars, owls.'

She read English at the University of Cambridge then moved to Abu Dhabi to help train hunting hawks for Arab sheikhs, before returning to teach at Cambridge. She wrote an academic history of falconry before writing *H is for Hawk*, a breathtaking blend of memoir and nature writing that became an instant bestseller. It won the Costa Book of the Year Award, the Prix du Meilleur Livre Étranger, and was the first ever memoir to win the Samuel Johnson Prize.

She has a regular column in the *New York Times* magazine and lives in Suffolk with a parrot called Birdoole. She still keeps three of Mabel's feathers in a jar on her desk.

H IS FOR HAWK

As a child, Helen Macdonald was determined to become a falconer, learning the arcane terminology and reading all the classic books. Years later, when her father died and she was struck deeply by grief, she became obsessed with the idea of training her own goshawk. She bought Mabel for £800 on a Scottish quayside and took her home to Cambridge, ready to embark on the long, strange business of trying to train this wildest of animals.

H is for Hawk is an unflinchingly honest account of Macdonald's struggle with grief during the difficult process of the hawk's taming and her own untaming. This is a book about memory, nature and nation, and how it might be possible to reconcile death with life and love.

'It just *sings*. I couldn't stop reading' Mark Haddon

'I can't remember the last time a book made me feel so many different things in such quick succession' Rachel Cooke, *Guardian*

'A soaring triumph' *Daily Telegraph*

VINTAGE MINIS

The Vintage Minis bring you the world's greatest writers on the experiences that make us human. These stylish, entertaining little books explore the whole spectrum of life – from birth to death, and everything in between. Which means there's something here for everyone, whatever your story.

vintageminis.co.uk